DATE DUE

DISCARD

# Marketing

*to*

# Moms

*Getting Your Share of the
Trillion-Dollar Market*

Maria T. Bailey

PRIMA PUBLISHING

To my children—Madison, Owen, Keenan, and Morgan—
who make me so proud to be their mother and to my
husband and best friend, Tim, who makes it all possible.

Published by Prima Publishing, Roseville, California. Member of the Crown Publishing Group, a division of Random House, Inc., New York.

PRIMA PUBLISHING and colophon are trademarks of Random House, Inc., reg-istered with the United States Patent and Trademark Office.

**Library of Congress Cataloging-in-Publication Data**
Bailey, Maria T.
    Marketing to moms : getting your share of the trillion-dollar market / Maria T. Bailey.
        p.    cm.
    Includes bibliographical references and index.
    ISBN 0-7615-6366-0
    1. Women consumers. 2. Mothers. 3. Marketing. I. Title.
HC79.C6 B295    2002
658.8'04—dc21                                              2002070443

02 03 04 05 QQ 10 9 8 7 6 5 4 3 2 1
Printed in the United States of America

First Edition

**Visit us online at www.primapublishing.com**

# Contents _____

# Acknowledgments ―――――――

IT DOESN T HAPPEN by accident that a working mother of four finds time to sit down—not to mention sit down and put her thoughts on paper. It is even more unlikely that a mother can find the uninterrupted time to sit and write an entire book. This book happened only through the efforts of a great many people, a few of whom I wish to acknowledge here.

I thank my husband, Tim, who stands behind me with love and support as I pursue my dreams and aspirations. Whether running a marathon or becoming a radio talk show host, Tim has been there to see me across the finish line.

I thank my children, Madison, Owen, Keenan, and Morgan, who had to share their mom with a computer and a list of chapters that hung on my office wall. Each night as I tucked Madison into bed, she would ask me for an update on the number of pages I had left to write. Keenan started each day with a simple question, "What chapter are you on now, Mom?", as he knew I stayed up writing well after he had gone to sleep. His only desire was that I finish this book quickly so that I might start writing a children's book with him. I'll never forget the day Owen came into my office to say, "Hey, Mom, you've been writing all day, why don't you give yourself a break?" The compassion expressed by my eight-year-old motivated me to press on. And Morgan, my three-year-old, managed only once to erase a chapter from my computer. I hope my writing has taught my children to be committed and dedicated to their passions in life.

Thank you to my business partner and very good friend, Rachael Bender. Together we have built a successful company from a dream. Few people possess her talents, and even fewer possess the qualities that make her special.

To the team of BlueSuitMom.com and BSM Media, thank you for all the dedication you demonstrate each day. Your contributions to this book and to our clients are appreciated immensely. Thank you to Judene Hartzell, also.

My appreciation goes to Randy Prange, Jack O'Hearn, and the team of Prange & O'Hearn Insights, Inc., for all their work in conducting and tabulating our moms' survey. Randy and I have traveled through many industries together. His wisdom and professional insights are invaluable.

I appreciate the time given by each marketing executive interviewed for this book. You don't reach the pinnacles these professionals have reached without a willingness to share ideas, insights, and advice. I'm grateful and happy they took the time to share it with me.

Thank you to our BSM Media clients who make working hard so fulfilling, especially Mark Dissette and Elizabeth Ostric.

There are many individuals who support you without even knowing they are doing so. They never realize how they positively touch your life because you never get around to thanking them. Well, the time is now, and I'd like to give them the thanks they deserve. To my good friends, Paige Hyatt, Pam Berrard, Jalima Huskey, Jill Botkin, Jill Oman, Marybeth Perry, Julie Marchese, Patti Campbell, Marti Zenor, Molly Gold, and Nancy DeJohn, thank you for being low maintenance friends whom I can always rely on for support. Thanks to two of the best moms I know, Brenda Kouwenhoven and Jennifer Calhoun. Every day as I sat at my computer, I watched Peggy Keating walk past my window. Her smile and constant words of kindness motivated me to keep typing, even when I wanted to stop. Last but not least, to Audrey Ring, who never lets me forget that anything is possible if you can bake brownies and run five miles before 7 A.M.

To my siblings: Debbi Jackson, Michael John Alligood, Mathew Alligood, Mike Redington, and Bryan Redington, who make being a big sister a special role. Thanks to my stepmother, Susan Telli, and my in-laws, Pat and Patrica Bailey, who always support me. Always in my thoughts is my stepfather, the late Dr. Michael Alligood, whose influence on my life is immeasurable. I only wish he was here to chat about it. To my mom, Jackie Alligood, thank you for all those times you sat with me late at night writing. You taught me how to express myself on paper. Thanks to my father, Bill Telli, who never let us forget the importance of setting priorities.

Thank you to Jennifer Basye Sander, who brought the idea for this book to life. Your insights are remarkable and forever amaze me. Thanks also to Andi Reese Brady, who made the toughest part of writing a book, dare I say it, fun—even on bad hair days.

Finally, to the many mothers who shared their thoughts, insights and opinions with me: Moms are busy people, but over 500 mothers took the time to be part of this book.

## www.marketingtomoms.com

Visit www.marketingtomoms.com, an interactive Web site offering a variety of services and resources for marketing professionals who want to tap into the mom market. To contact Maria Bailey about consulting with your company or speaking at your next strategy meeting or sales conference, call (954) 943-2322 or e-mail her at maria@bsmmedia.com.

# Introduction ─────────────────

I

T'S A SUNNY Saturday morning, and children laugh as
they travel down a big, twisted Rubbermaid slide. A
young school-age girl wearing the latest spring coordinates
from Target dangles from the monkey bars. Two boys in
Oakley shades throw a Wilson leather football in the grass
while their baby sister sits in her bright blue Peg Perego
stroller chewing on Cheerios and sipping Mott's Apple
Juice. Four mothers sit on a bench chatting, faces made up
with Avon. One shares Kodak moments from a recent
Disney vacation while another looks up from her *"O"* magazine just in time to see her son jump from a not-so-low
branch. The moms range in age from early twenties to late
forties, and each is wearing her own interpretation of casual
wear. Six Schwinn bikes of various sizes line the fence, and a
lone pair of Nike shoes sits by the sandbox. A Good Humor
ice cream truck slowly drives down the adjacent street. Ah,
yes, it's Saturday morning in the park.

In order to best appreciate the awesome power of
mothers as consumers, simply visit a popular park in your
town. Within minutes of sitting next to a sandbox you'll hear
mothers compare health coverage, gather input on baby
foods, critique the hottest family vacation destinations, and

utter their two cents on the latest political race. Their toddlers (adorned in Oshkosh overalls, Old Navy t-shirts, or Disney-licensed clothing) play nearby. Lined along the sidewalk is an assortment of Peg Perego strollers and Little Tikes riding toys. It is all a brilliant example of the spending power of mothers. From the diapers on their babies to the chicken they serve for dinner to the minivans that line the parking lot, moms spend money and, thankfully for consumer marketers, moms love to talk about where they spend it.

Back in the park, a group of mothers stands chatting as they push their preschoolers on the swings. They are an example of the most powerful marketing tool in existence—word of mouth, or as I like to call it, "word of mom." In no other segment of consumers is word of mouth more powerful. Mothers love to talk, compare, and share. If you've won the admiration of a mother, you can be assured she'll spread the word. The many ways to reach mothers with your marketing message is the primary focus of this book. We'll look at the mom market up close, from top to bottom.

It should come as no surprise that it was in a park that I discovered some of the ideas that gave rise to this book. I often visit city parks to maintain a pulse on what I refer to as the "mom market." Although my mother taught me that eavesdropping is impolite, it serves as my best source of market research. I recently sat building sand castles with my toddler, Morgan, and listened to three mothers evaluate Disney's newest theme park, Animal Kingdom. As one mother detailed every aspect of her recent visit to Orlando, the other two mothers listened attentively and asked for hotel, restaurant, and car-rental recommendations. Within a three-minute conversation, five different consumer brands were given the seal of approval by a happy mom—and two other families became customers.

Just think, if the average family spends $250 on car rentals in Orlando, the rental car company just made $500 the next time these two satisfied moms travel to Disney World. Now picture 100 satisfied mothers sitting in parks throughout the country recommending your rental car company. That's potentially 200 new customers for a total of $50,000 in incremental revenue. The best part is that acquiring these new customers essentially costs the company nothing. What marketing executive would rather pay $50,000 for a full-page ad in a national parenting publication than have 100 moms talking about his or her product on park benches? The return on investment will quickly illustrate that having moms talk positively about your product is the best form of advertising.

Why do I spend so much time in parks observing mothers? Besides being the mother of four young children who love afternoons on the monkey bars and swings, I do it for my clients. As the CEO of BSM Media, Inc. (www.bsm media.com), a full-service media and marketing company that specializes in connecting clients with the mom market; cofounder of BlueSuitMom.com, an award-winning Web site designed for executive working mothers; and host of "Mom Talk Radio," South Florida's first radio show for busy moms, it's literally my job to know the issues that are important to mothers. I bring a unique combination of personal and professional experience in the mom market to my clients. In addition to this book, I share many of my tips, findings, and experience with marketing executives on www .marketingtomoms.com. I invite you to visit the Web site and sign up for the free e-mail newsletter, filled with the latest on the mom market.

I remember when Discovery Zone play centers were my client and I had three babies under the age of twenty months at home. I spent many a day sitting in colored ball pits with my children in one arm and writing press releases with the other. My personal experience gives me a unique perspective on my professional goals. I've been fortunate enough to merge my personal and professional passions.

I know what it feels like to walk the aisle of Target with four children in tow, but I also appreciate the challenge of a marketer in capturing 30 seconds of a busy mom's attention. Most important, I've witnessed the financial impact that successfully creating a buzz in the mom market can make for my clients. The bottom line is that mothers represent trillions of dollars in spending. Capturing even a small portion of that spending can deliver dollars to your bottom line.

I believe so much in the informal market research of a park visit that I recently suggested to a client that they toss aside a fancy and expensive market research proposal and host a cookie break at a park. I can't take the credit for the idea. It was a concept executed by Amilya Antonetti of SoapWorks. When launching SoapWorks, Antonetti placed an ad in a local San Francisco newspaper that read, "Calling All Moms: Mom looking to start a company, and I need your help. If you could create your perfect cleaning solution and body-care products, what would they look like? Providing free lunch, guaranteed entertainment. Bring your kids." More than 220 mothers turned out to share their ideas and insights. Antonetti's cost was less than a hundred dollars. The same focus group project could have cost her thousands of dollars had she hired a big-name firm—and given her less valuable results.

You don't have to host a major event for moms to gain valuable information. A quick glimpse at the park parking lot will tell you not only the popular makes and models of the vehicles moms are buying, but also color preferences, frequency of car purchases, and favorite features. Chances are that a particular logo adorns the clothes of more than one child climbing on the jungle gym. There is a lot to be learned about the buying power of a mother.

# A Trillion-Dollar Market

RECENT U.S. STATISTICS show that the mother in the family controls 80 percent of all household spending.[1] (In families represented by a single mother, this percentage is of course considerably higher.) This number represents $1.6 trillion in spending—utopia for consumer product and service companies.[2] Single mothers alone account for $174 billion in annual spending.[3] Some companies discovered the power of the mom market many years ago. For example, Avon and Tupperware have built retail empires selling to moms and have even leveraged the power of the mom network by employing mothers to sell their product.

Mothers are easily the most important consumer group in markets that include household and personal care products and packaged goods. Their influence goes beyond purchases at the grocery store. They shop for tools, toiletries, plumbers, investment accounts, office supplies, airline tickets, cars, pets, and, of course, houses. They buy soccer balls, sod, snowblowers, food, books, videos, vacations, toys, and pay tuition. Moms spend money.

Moms are not only controlling household spending, they are spending money in business as well. Women, many of whom are mothers, are starting an estimated 4 million businesses a year.[4] They are buying office supplies, copiers, faxes, computers, and accounting and legal services. Mothers, looking for a way to balance a career and family, are starting home-based businesses at four times the rate of their male counterparts.[5] These companies range from small one-person service providers to multimillion-dollar businesses. Women employed outside the home control $1.5 trillion in spending for business.[6] This spending is coming not just from mothers in business for themselves but from mothers employed by others.

A Census Bureau report cites that even among mothers with very young children, more than 60 percent are in the labor force.[7] A typical middle manager will decide where her department goes for a celebration luncheon, or how to budget advertising expenses, or whether to send a colleague to an out-of-town meeting. Administrative assistants and bookkeepers order millions of dollars of office supplies a month.

With over 25 million mothers in the workplace, companies must now also market themselves as an employer of choice to working mothers.[8] We will discuss the types of benefits that attract and retain mothers as employees in greater detail in chapter 11. Moms are making their voices heard in the halls of government, too. Although it is not necessary to capture the heart of every voting mother to win an election, it is impossible to win without a majority of them. Mothers represent an important block of votes for candidates, particularly those running for president. The so-called soccer

# Mom's Money

■ According to the U.S. Department of Agriculture (the agency that tracks family expenditures), an average-income family will spend $165,630 on a child by the time the child reaches eighteen years of age.[10]

■ Parents with incomes of $38,000 to $64,000 spent $18,510 on miscellaneous items for the average child from birth through the age of eighteen. This includes spending on entertainment, reading material, VCRs, summer camps, and lessons.[11]

■ Females outnumber males in the United States by over six million (roughly 6 percent) and a significant percent have at least one child. There are 141 million women in the United States; 73 million of them have children.[12]

■ There are 6.2 million woman-owned businesses in the United States.[13]

■ Woman-owned businesses generate $1.15 trillion in sales.[14]

■ Women-owned businesses employ 9.2 million people.[15]

■ U.S. women spend more than $3.7 trillion annually on consumer goods and services, plus another $1.5 trillion as purchasing agents for businesses. As a group U.S. women constitute the number three market in the world, with their collective buying power exceeding the economy of Japan.[16]

■ Eighty percent of all checks written in the United States are signed by women.[17]

mom contingent helped put Bill Clinton in the White House in 1996. In the last four presidential elections, suburban mothers have represented one-fifth of all the votes cast.[9]

In order to capture a portion of the trillions of dollars spent by mothers, you must recognize the power of mothers, appreciate the time they put into selecting a product, and understand what it means to be a mother in the twenty-first century.

## Marketers Talk About the Mom Market

■ Terry Whaples, president, Holiday Inn Family Suites: "My team and I believe that the mother is the backbone in the family. If mothers don't travel, no one travels. If we don't satisfy mothers we are not going to get their sales."

■ Tom Gruber, former vice president of International Marketing, McDonald's, and chief marketing officer, Blockbuster Video: "Mothers control the buying power of children. . . . Without the awareness of the mothers, children have no access to your products."

■ Neil Closner, CEO of BabyUniverse.com: "The benefit of a mother as a customer is that she hangs out with other mothers who are basically in the same demographic group who are buying the same products at the same time she is. You can guess that a mother of a two year old is spending her time with other mothers of two year olds and they will all need potty-training supplies at about the same time. . . . Moms deliver other mothers to your business."

■ Stephanie Azzarone, president of Child's Play Communications: "Moms not only decide what to purchase for themselves, they are also the key decision makers

when it comes to family/household purchases
majority of time, it's moms who decide what a
going to eat, how a home is going to be furnisl
everyone is going on vacation, and just about every
other aspect of family life."

■ Marilyn O'Brien, president of Marketing Moms:
"Moms are the key driving force for purchase decisions
for their family. . . . Think about it, how many times do
you think a man yells to his wife, 'While you're at the
store would you mind picking me up a can of after-
shave?' I know from my own buying experience that unless he is brand-sensitive, I will pick up the product that
has my personal appeal."

## What's in This Book

IN THE PAGES to follow, we will examine some of the most
successful marketing initiatives used to attract mothers to a
product, identify a few that don't work, and even discuss a
few that offend mothers. My goal was to assemble ideas and
information that could be applied to any size marketing
budget by any size company. We will hear from some of the
top marketing executives in the country. I've gathered the insights and experiences of a diverse and respected group of
marketing professionals from large consumer brands, such as
Alamo Rent A Car and Blockbuster, to smaller niche companies, such as Go Mom Inc., and Amazingmoms.com. None
of these companies can survive without the mom market. For
some, as you will see, that lesson was learned the hard way.

In addition to presenting my own personal advice and tips of
how to market to mothers, I decided to go directly to other moms
across the country for their advice. With the assistance of Prange

& O'Hearn Insights, Inc., we surveyed and interviewed over 500 mothers from across the United States. We asked questions about the advertising messages that drive them to buy a product, direct mail pieces they keep or throw away, publications they read, and where they go on the Web to make purchases for themselves and their family. The survey results represent single moms, working mothers, stepmothers, new moms, and so on—in short, just about every type of mom.

The results of our findings, along with the anecdotal comments of real-life mothers, fill the pages of chapter 12. I think you will find them interesting, informative, and, in some instances, surprising. (A full copy of this survey can be obtained from Prange & O'Hearn Insights, Inc., by calling 772-223-9223 or visiting www.marketingtomoms.com.)

This is the first time that anyone has paired the insights of leading marketers with a survey of mothers on the subject of marketing to moms. There will be times, as in real life, when the two sides don't agree. It's a perfect illustration of why some ads miss their targets. Digest the information and apply it in a way that works for you. Moms do it every day as they juggle the challenges of balancing parenthood and life.

Perhaps that's the first thing we should learn from the mom market: There's not a right or wrong way of doing it, just the best way for you and your company. Let's begin our task of learning how to capture a piece of the trillion-dollar mom market.

## CHAPTER ONE

# Understanding the Mom Market

M OM. MOMMY. MA. Mama. . . . Ask a person to describe a mother and the answers will vary as much as
the words people use to identify her. Mothers come in
shapes and sizes that go beyond their physical appearance.

Few things are as constant in life as mothers—everyone
has had one at some time. Along with having a mother
comes an emotional tie. For some, this tie may conjure up
pleasant memories, and in others it may evoke feelings of
distress, sadness, or confusion. Marketers' definition of a
mother can be clouded by personal experience with their
own mothers. To further confuse the issue, observations of
mothers around them and their own experience as mothers
may contribute to their definition. Herein lies the challenge
of characterizing mothers.

## Complexity and Variety

MOLLY GOLD, FOUNDER of Go Mom, Inc., and creator
of the Go Mom Planner, describes a mother this way: "In

a word, phenomenal! We see her strengths as unconditionally committed, spiritually inquisitive, endlessly loving, smart, busy, conscientious, fun, savvy, responsible, frugal, value oriented, morally concerned, politically aware, charitably motivated, effectively organized, child development enthusiast and a brilliant imaginative play coordinator." Gold continues her characterization of a mother by describing her challenges: "She is tired, frequently overwhelmed, can fret with the sacrifices both financial and emotional of giving up her previous career or fret with the intense challenge of managing two full-time jobs, has higher expectations of herself than anyone else around her, might not ask for help often enough, might not take the initiative to provide herself with a regular break from her responsibilities to recharge, and would love to see clothes in the misses department that are both stylish and respectable for a body that has given birth and not quite found the time to find its best new shape."

Avon showed us in new advertising that most of today's moms don't idolize June Cleaver anymore. These ads featured tennis stars Venus and Serena Williams and spoke to a woman who believes self-image is important. The ads suggested that Avon understands that today's moms have new ideals of beauty and celebrity.

Kit Bennet, president of Amazingmoms.com and mother of three, defines moms by what they aren't anymore as well. "Moms are no longer the cookie-baking, nose-wiping, shirt-ironing moms of the past. They are working both in and out of the homes. However, I believe that moms feel guilty that they may not be meeting the traditional roles, so they try to combine both. My market is mothers who are busy either at work or with their family and want to do it all—spend quality time with their families, give spectacular parties, and still maintain their individuality."

Maria F. Soldani—executive director of Marketing and Public Relations for Holy Cross Hospital in Fort Lauderdale, mother of two, and grandmother—believes that a mother by today's definition is an *artist*. "She must compose and orchestrate her family's activities. She designs and builds relationships with her children and their peers. Today's mother also sculpts and molds the morals, ethics, and spirituality of her family. She paints events, celebrations, and quiet times with a full palette of hues that cover the spectrum of her talents as a woman. Today's mother is an evolutionary woman who, through personal and professional growth, has achieved balance in her life. The mother keeps growing in wisdom and experience as the children's needs decrease and her personal development continues to increase."

It would be easy for me, as the mother of four, to assume that I know what a mother is and what a mother wants in her goods and services. But a closer examination of myself as a mother would illustrate that I am many types of mother. I am an adoptive mother. I am a working mother, a mother of young children, a Southern mother, and a Catholic mother. Each of these "types" of mothers carries its own separate beliefs, values, challenges, and perceptions of the world. I've never been one to think I was a complicated person, but attach the word "mother" to my identity and I suddenly assume a complex personality.

You can slice and dice moms a hundred ways. There are working moms, stay-at-home moms, part-time moms, moms who are business owners, home-based working mothers, new moms, experienced moms, first-time moms—the list goes on and on. The mom market can also be defined by its children.

Moms of toddlers are different from the moms of teens. Moms of twins differ from moms of only children. Where a mother is in her life when she becomes a mother creates differences. Single mothers have different needs than married mothers and older mothers vary from teen mothers.

A fundamental rule of marketing is to know your market. I like to take it one step further and say that it is important to not only know your market but to know what it is like to walk in the shoes of your customer. It has been written many times that Dave Thomas, the late founder of the Wendy's restaurant chain, ate a cheeseburger and a bowl of chili everyday for lunch. This allowed Dave to know exactly the quality of the food that his customers experienced in his restaurants. When Blockbuster Video was headquartered in Fort Lauderdale, Florida, it was not uncommon to find Wayne Huizenga, founder and former CEO, browsing the titles of the new releases on a Friday night. He explained his actions by saying that if he expected his customers to truly experience "Wow, what a difference!" he had to experience it firsthand himself. On the same note, he had to know the frustration of *not* finding the newest release on the shelf in order to implement inventory policies that keep the hottest hits available to customers. You have to know your customers' experiences to truly know how to meet their needs.

## Defining Moms

IN ORDER TO define "mother," we must examine the physical features as well as the emotional attributes that comprise a mom.

## BIOLOGY

To begin our search for a definition of a mother, let's start with biology. Dr. Gail Gross (nationally known expert on child development and behavior and host of the radio show, "Let's Talk,") encourages marketers to remember that mothers are living organisms. A mother is a thinking and feeling female who has procreated and delivered offspring. She possesses all the natural behaviors that come along with having offspring, such as nurturing, caring, and protecting it.

"You have to remember when you are dealing with mothers that you can't cut them off at the neck," she says. "You have to appeal to their brain as well as their hearts. Their logic is as important as their emotions." Gross adds that in the simplest definition we are all just sexual primates. We are born, we procreate, we nurture our young, and then we are on borrowed time until our life ends. Not much separates us from any other mammal when it comes to being a mother except one major difference. We spend a lot of money on our offspring. Some estimate that we spend more than $100,000 on them in the first three years of life.[1]

The starting place for defining a mother is a common ground. It is safe to begin with the following: moms are reproductive primates with the capacity to think and feel. Unfortunately for marketers and those who control advertising budgets, that's about where the commonality ends. From this point on, it is almost impossible to keep all mothers in one population. It is important to segment the market, to decide what subpopulation is important to your business or brand, and to understand what makes them tick. They might all be women with children but they are more complex than that.

## A MOSAIC OF INFLUENCES

I asked every person I interviewed for this book to characterize a mother for me. As you might expect, I got a variety of answers. The best answer came from Bonnie Ulman, cofounder and principal with The Haystack Group, a consumer research firm based in Atlanta, Georgia. Ulman's company, which she began with her partner, a counseling psychologist, was created because they were disillusioned with the way marketers were attaching labels to people without recognizing that they were multi-dimensional human beings. "A mother is like a mosaic and you have to have all the tiles in place to get a true picture of who she is," explains Ulman.

Each of the tiles that make up a mother can be traced to a personal experience, attitude, memory of her own mother, and what Ulman refers to as "parenting style." The latter, she believes, is the most important element to identify when trying to characterize the mothers you intend to market your product to.

"First, you have to look at the population as a subpopulation, but it is important to recognize parenting style. It is critical to understand because it speaks volumes to what has happened in their life and how they will respond to a brand or an issue," explains Ulman, a mother of two. "Parenting style is a reflection of personality and characteristics and like the colors of a mosaic tends to go from one side of the spectrum to the other. One extreme of the mosaic is the mother who maintains her own identity separate from her children and that of being a mother. She has goals and the challenges her motherhood presents are conquered like other goals in her life. She is the one who is more about selfness. In advertising, this is the take-no-prisoners mom. The other end of the spectrum is the mother who relishes her children to the point that she has no individual identity. She has a difficult time letting go and understanding that life with children is messy, scheduling is crazy, and there are going to be bumps in the road. As a marketer, you have to find the best place on the spectrum and decide what you promise to the mother with that particular parenting style."

Secondly, Ulman adds, you must look at the circumstances at the moment that you are trying to get to her. For example, look at two mothers in the same demographic with the same income level and same number of children. If one is single or working outside the home, she will react differently than a mother who is married and not working outside the home.

Perhaps because Ulman is the mother of two children herself and most likely reads *The Velveteen Rabbit* as a bedtime story, she likes to illustrate her ideas by using a "Velveteen mother." In *The Velveteen Rabbit,* the stuffed toy rabbit comes into the nursery unaware of what is real and what is not. He turns to the Skin Horse, an old, experienced toy who educates him throughout the book. The Velveteen Rabbit dreams of becoming a real rabbit one day. Like the rabbit in the story, which starts out not knowing anything about what is real in life, mothers enter motherhood with little knowledge of the realities of motherhood. This is a fortunate circumstance for us marketers because this is where "word of mom" begins. New moms begin asking what name, what bottles, what stroller? In *The Velveteen Rabbit,* the rabbit turns to the Skin Horse to provide him with answers. New moms, or Velveteen mothers per Ulman, will ask experienced mothers for the answers to their questions. If you have Skin Horses talking about you, they are likely to recommend your product to these new moms. The challenge for us as advertisers is that we must position our message in terms that the mother can understand. Are your moms Velveteen mothers or Skin Horses? If you position your message over or under them, you don't make an electric connection and without the electric connection you can't develop a loyal relationship. You want marketing to create a relationship.

## LIFE STAGES (A.K.A. CHANGE POINTS)

Up to now we have characterized our mom as a living organism who has emotion and logic and has developed a parenting style that was influenced by her community, personality, and attitudes. Ulman expands her characterization of a mother by incorporating a third essential element: life-course development, which is based on the idea that human beings can be expected to unfold in a certain process. You can expect that babies will walk at about twelve months and that a toddler will start talking at about twenty-four months. A woman might have a meltdown on her thirtieth birthday and a bigger one at forty. The psychosocial things happening to us at each of these stages influence them. What is happening around us impacts our development. You might feel like you're still a teenager, but a babysitter calling you "sir" or "ma'am" will remind you that you are really forty.

Marilyn O'Brien, president of Marketing Moms and former Procter and Gamble marketing executive, agrees with Ulman that marketing to moms sharing a life stage (a similar point in time as it relates to living life) is important. O'Brien however prefers to call it marketing to "change points."

"Change points are times in a mother's life when big things happen. It might be initially becoming a mother and now there is a struggle about working and assuming a role of caretaker. Another change point occurs when the children go off to school and a mother becomes an empty nester. Or when a mother goes through menopause. These things can have a major impact on what they are feeling as a woman and in their role as a mother."

To successfully market to various change points, it is important to recognize the subsets of each segment. For example, if you are targeting mothers raising babies and toddlers, you need to segment by mindset just as Ulman did with her Velveteen mother illustration. A first-time mother has a different mindset than an experienced mother of a newborn. The first-time mother has a high anxiety level and as a marketer you need to build her confidence as a mom and in your product. As the anxiety-ridden new mother evolves, so does her thinking. You as a marketer must know where her head is when she is receiving your message.

Some products do not require you to split hairs and whittle down to life stages. Snack items, cereals, and produce don't have to market to life stages because they appeal to a larger market. However, if you want to send a specific message, such as Cheerios are good snacks that toddlers can't choke on, then again you would need to segment your marketing initiative down to a life stage.

## LIFESTYLE GROUPS

Any particular combination of the many mosaic pieces made up by change points, attitudes, personalities, and experiences can put a mother in a subgroup known as a "lifestyle group." This is where you walk in the shoes of your mom market. As an experienced mom myself, I suggest you grab a pair of your best jogging shoes because if you are going to be following a mom, you'll be doing lots of running. Moms, regardless of their lifestyle group, rarely stand still.

Moms who share a lifestyle group are mothers that share the same daily routines. This doesn't mean that every working mother makes breakfast at 6 A.M., packs lunches at 7 A.M., and leaves for the office at 8 A.M. Rather, a lifestyle group shares the same daily components, such as dividing time between the office and the home, and similar goals. In the case of working mothers, one important goal is balancing work and family. Women who work in a home office have different challenges and consumer needs than mothers who teach school each day. It is important to recognize those differences before formulating a marketing plan for your product or company.

You can effectively market to more than one lifestyle group as long as you appeal to the common threads that join the various subgroups. For instance, safety is an issue important to mothers in almost all subgroups. The trick is to present the message in a way that can speak to mothers at different change points. You won't talk about keeping your child safe in the same way to stay-at-home new mothers as you would to working mothers of teens.

Marketing to moms seems so complicated. It reminds me of my days as a biology major and the hours I spent in a chemistry lab learning what elements could be mixed in a test tube without causing an explosion. The same reaction can happen if you mix the wrong message with the wrong segment of mothers. A marketing initiative with the wrong message can go up in flames and take your brand with it.

## TRADITIONALISTS AND ME-MOMS

To help make the mom market a little less complicated, some marketers have tried to create neatly packaged groups of mothers. As you are about to learn, not all marketers see moms the same.

Bruce Tait, managing partner for Fallon Brand Consulting, a firm that specializes in brand strategy development, has represented many of American's best-known brands, including Lee Jeans and General Mills. He is also a frequent speaker at the International Association of Marketing Professionals.

"We have had a great deal of experience with branding for mothers. First, we have seen that you can't treat all mothers the same. You must segment the mother category. We see two separate groups of mothers: traditionalists and me-moms."

Traditionalists, Tait explains, are mothers that tend to be willing to be at home nurturing their families. They believe that their current sacrifices are for the betterment of their children and household and they gain their joy from doing for others. They have children because they want to raise and nurture children and give them their love. They want products that will give them enough freedom to add their own special touch to it. For instance, they might like the ease of a three-step cake mix but they also like that it allows them to add their own special touches to the icing and decorations.

The other group that Tait identifies he calls the "me-moms." "They have a different perspective on having children. They have children to gain the love of a child. They love their children and want the best for them but they also like motherhood to be easy. Even though they want their children to have good, healthy meals, they need ease in preparing meals. They want convenience. Much to our surprise, the me-mom market is significant in size," Tait adds.

"It might sound insensitive to compare these mothers to consumers in the pet category but there is an overlap in the way people think about nurturing. We have seen it in working with clients like Purina. There is one group of pet-product consumers that love their pet and want to give it the best life possible. The other group has a pet in order to gain the love a dog or cat can give them," explains Tait.

The traditionalist and me-moms are represented in all ages and life stages of mothers. It appears that the difference between the two is not a stage but more an ingrained approach to motherhood than anything else.

The challenge to marketing professionals is that in communicating with these two groups, you must be cautious. An advertising campaign that speaks too much to one group may alienate the other. The me-mom can view the same ad as a traditionalist yet gain a completely different message. This can be seen in reactions to the infamous AT&T ad where the working mother is rushing around the kitchen to get out the door to an office meeting. Her daughter asks when she can schedule a meeting and the next scene is the mother on the beach with her daughter, doing business on her cell phone as her daughter plays in the surf. I always applauded this particular commercial; in fact I believed it depicted my internal struggle as a working mother to a tee and it made me feel good every time I watched it. So you can imagine my surprise when some mothers told me they hated this commercial. I didn't understand why until I watched the commercial again, this time wearing the shoes of a traditionalist.

In my newfound role as a traditionalist mother, I could not relate to why the AT&T mother would value time away from her children and I certainly didn't approve of her being on her cell phone when she was supposed to be enjoying an outing to the beach with her daughter. In fact, I was almost angry at AT&T for creating a device that interrupted a mother's time with her child. Thus, my favorite commercial as a working mother trying to find products to help me juggle work and family took on a totally different appearance when I viewed it as a stay-at-home mother.

# Narrowing the Definitions Further: LeoBurnett's LeoShe Studies

NO ONE EVER said marketing was easy. Just as those in the marketplace can disagree on how they view marketers' messages, marketers themselves disagree on characterizing the segments.

Denise Fedewa is senior vice president and director of Strategic Planning for LeoBurnett, one of the world's largest advertising firms, representing over 200 full-service advertising agencies and a variety of specialty marketing services. She has spent a large portion of her career studying women and headed a 1999 study by LeoShe, a team at LeoBurnett dedicated to women's issues.

Fedewa agrees that ignoring the complexity of motherhood is detrimental to the advertisers' bottom line: to sell. People won't buy products, she reminds us, unless they can fit them into their ideal image of what their lives should be like.

Fedewa dispels the importance of the impact of generation and life stages when characterizing mothers. "We have done five studies on women. Each one we went into with the hypothesis that life stage and generation must have something to do with the way you market to a mother."

The team at LeoShe set out to dig deeper into the market than any marketers had ever dug before. They were on a mission, Fedewa says, to throw out all the old clichés and stereotypical generalizations of mothers and to segment beyond the stay-at-home versus working mother categories. LeoShe's research was a combination of cultural audits where they looked at how mothers were being portrayed in the media, on television, and in ads and focus groups. They conducted "girlfriend groups," a type of focus group where they gathered a small group of friends together in a familiar living room to chat about their views.

Regarding their hypothesis about generational and life stages being a uniting factor among moms, Fedewa explains that when her team started each study, they would set up the research based on this hypothesis. Motivated to find generational differences, they examined generation X moms versus baby boomer moms. (The girlfriend groups tended to be groups of generation Xers and groups of baby boomers.)

Fedewa says that they could find no differences between the two generations. They did, however, find two other contributors to a woman's attitude toward motherhood.

## SELF-ACTUALIZATION AND THE INVOLVEMENT OF FATHERS

"The mother's need for self-actualization and her view of the father's involvement trumped generational factors," says Fedewa. "Four distinct groups of mothers evolved based on common thoughts related to these two elements."

Before we look at the four groups that Fedewa's research uncovered, let's look at these two variables more closely.

"Self-actualization" is the term that Fedewa and her team used to describe the extent to which women were still pursuing their interests outside of their role as a mother. They found that some women get all their needs for self-esteem and self-actualization from the motherhood role. They see their role and job in life as a mother and it becomes their identity. Other women find that they have a need to fulfill themselves with jobs, titles, and identities outside of motherhood.

In a time when more mothers are working and assuming multiple roles in their lives, it is important to identify the potential marketing opportunities that can be realized by recognizing a woman's self-actualization. Consider the 6.2 million women who own businesses.[2] If an office supply company acknowledged that these women were not only mothers but also women who took pride in running their own businesses, they could likely capture incremental sales by gaining these mothers as business customers as well as family consumers. Where do you think they will shop next September for back-to-school supplies? The answer is the business that valued them in the same manner that they valued themselves: as female business owners as well as mothers.

Involvement of the father was the second important value to emerge from the LeoShe research. Involvement includes how much the father helps emotionally, physically, and financially in raising the children. Interestingly enough, it was the mom's *perception* of the father's involvement that mattered, not how much the father was involved in reality. For example, many moms responded that their husbands were equal partners even when in actuality they were not. This variable becomes tricky to navigate especially since a 2000 Census Bureau report cited that the fastest growing demographic in the United States today is single mothers. For the first time, the number of single-person households is greater than the number of nuclear families. Single-mother families increased from 3 million in 1970 to 10 million in 2000.[3] You might assume that the number of single mothers is growing because divorce rates continue to grow but the reality is that many are electing to become single moms.[4] Forty-one percent of unmarried-partner households included children under eighteen, just slightly less than the proportion of married-couple households with children under eighteen (46 percent).[5]

The number of people cohabiting doubled over the past decade, to 5.4 million. Between 1970 and 1999, the percentage of children in two-parent families decreased for all races. The number of Hispanic children living in two-parent families decreased from 78 percent to 63 percent. The percentage of African American children in two-parent families declined from 58 percent to 35 percent, and the number of white children in two-parent homes decreased from 90 percent to 74 percent.[6]

The roles that fathers are playing in the lives of their children are varied in their levels of involvement. But regardless of where the father is in the relationship with the mother, most mothers would like the father to be involved with the child.

Fedewa's team found that women in every group liked to see father involvement in advertisements. It doesn't always represent reality but it does represent a dream for mothers. There is a feeling that if my husband or the father of my child sees this, maybe he will take on the role being portrayed in the ad and it will come true.

## THE FOUR LEOSHE GROUPS

With the combination of self-actualization and perception of the father's involvement as a common denominator, Fedewa and her team found four distinct groups.

### June Cleaver: The Sequel

"The first group was called 'The June Cleaver: The Sequel,' which was the most traditional group," says Fedewa. These women have the most traditional gender roles in terms of their jobs in the family. "The Sequel" was attached to the name because these mothers are living in the twenty-first century and the circumstances are different and they must deal with that in their lives. These mothers believe that mothers of young children should not work; but about 50 percent of these women are working—many part-time. The work aspect is part of the "sequel" tag, an outward sign that times have changed and that today a vast number of women work by choice or out of necessity.

These mothers also feel that their need for self-actualization is fulfilled in motherhood. They feel that the fathers of their children are involved but in an interesting way: The father comes home from work and plays with the kids and he does activities with the kids on the weekends. But let's clarify that although they consider the father to be involved, this is not a father who's staying home with a sick child or running the car pool. The June Cleaver mother is okay with his level of involvement because her definition of their roles is that it is his job to make money and her job to take care of the kid stuff.

Fedewa adds that these moms tend to be Caucasian and high income. "They are educated and most have a college degree." Many marketers, she adds, fall into the trap that they have to use images of June Cleaver types in ads targeting these moms. But it isn't necessary to play back people's lives to them in your ads. You just need to give them cues that you understand their life.

As a fictitious example, let's say you are selling brooms. You might find that the most compelling thing to your target is that when you sweep with this broom, there's not a single speck of dirt left. You don't need to show any person at all in this ad. You just want to prove that this broom picks dirt up better than any other broom. You might know from your research that this message is more important to working mothers (who don't have time to re-sweep the floor when a broom misses a few specks) than it is to the June Cleaver types but you don't need to show either type of woman in the ad.

## Tug of War

Fedewa calls the next group "Tug of War." "These women have many of the same beliefs as 'June Cleaver: The Sequel,' however, their income level is low and they cannot live that lifestyle. They're pretty upset about it. They're angry with their spouses. They feel like the father is not helping with the work of raising their children and there's also some resentment because he's not supporting the family enough," says Fedewa. This working woman is guilty, harried, and stressed-out. She resents working outside the home and the time away from her children, and further, she's the one who has to come home and do the whole second shift because nothing's happened during the day. Demographically, the "Tug of War" group is certainly lower income but Denise's team saw no skew to age or ethnicity. Close to 90 percent were working mothers.

"In order to market to these mothers, you have to show ideals that relieve their angst. You have to be supportive but recognize that not everything is perfect. These mothers want to nurture their children but they are consumed by tasks in life. Marketers can reach these mothers by playing to the fact that these mothers will buy products that provide mothering," explains Fedewa.

## Strong Shoulders

The third group that emerged, "Strong Shoulders," is interesting because they have a lot of the same circumstances as the Tug of War women: lower income, little support from the father of their children—in fact a lot of them are single moms. Strong Shoulders have to work but they don't hold the June Cleaver model up as what they're supposed to be doing, so they're okay with the fact that they're working. Strong Shoulders have a "I'm going to make the best of this situation" kind of outlook.

Fedewa says that women who came into motherhood in an unexpected way drove this group: in LeoShe's research groups 89 percent of them said their first pregnancy was unplanned versus 40 percent for the stay-at-home moms. This group skews younger. Thirty percent of them were eighteen to twenty-four.

### Mothers of Invention

In Fedewa's last group, "Mothers of Invention," are women who come right out and say that the father is an equal partner in raising the children. These dads would stay home with a sick child, run car pool, and do errands. Mothers of Invention enjoy their work and the outlet that it gives them. They feel well rounded. Adds Fedewa, "It's probably easier for them to feel that way because the dads are so involved and many have good support networks beyond the dads."

This group was skewed toward upper income but not as strongly as June Cleaver: The Sequel. There was evidence of this kind of mom in all income groups. At the time of the research this group seemed to be taking advantage of technology and the labor shortage to invent creative, flexible working arrangements.

## SHIFTS IN CONTRIBUTING FACTORS: SEPTEMBER 11

Although Fedewa says the four segments defined in her 1999 research still apply to mothers today, she adds that the events of September 11, 2001, could shift some of the contributing factors within each group.

"Ironically when we used to present the results of our research, we would always preface it with a disclaimer of sorts that these were results that could be applied to the mom's market barring unforeseen disasters that might drastically change the world we live in and impact the attitudes of mothers. The week after September 11, it happened. Now we wait to see the fallout of the events," says Fedewa. "The Strong Shoulders may become a shrinking group now that the job market is not as strong and people are rethinking their priorities. When the economy was booming and employers were willing to make all sort of interesting arrangements to get good employees—flex, telecommuting, and job sharing—this group thrived. Today, I don't know that employers are as motivated to do these things because there is a flood of good full-time people in the market for a job."

One general effect of September 11 that will play a part in shaping mothers is internal reflection on individual priorities. Country music singer Alan Jackson describes it perfectly in his hit song, "Where Were You When the World Stopped Turning?" One line in the song asks if you called your mother or hugged your children. Both men and women wanted to be close to their families post September 11. That trend continues. People are deciding to stay closer to home, be happier with less, and find solutions that simplify their lives.

You can see the effects in the increase in home-based businesses springing up since September 2001. Women-owned businesses grew by 37 percent from 1997 to 2002—four times the growth rate of all firms, with 28 percent of them being home-based businesses.[7] This may be due to many contributing factors, but I believe that women who were considering going back to work outside the home prior to September 2001 may have reevaluated their options afterward.

In an *American Demographics* survey of 2,532 adults, conducted between October 9 and 11, 2001, 80 percent said that the attacks have increased their appreciation of families and 69 percent said that family is a greater priority now than before September 11, 2001.[8] Reprioritizing home and family has caused a resurgence of Hallmark card moments such as reconnecting with long lost family members, finding additional quality time, and staying in touch with loved ones when you have to be apart.

## Recognizing What Matters

A CLEAR AND positive element for advertisers and marketers to recognize post September 11 is that moms, regardless of the label they wear, are more committed than ever to finding a solution to their struggle to balance their lives. There is an opportunity for marketers to speak to a mother's desire to simplify her household chores, serve family dinners, experience memorable moments with her children, and keep the things she values close to her.

Ironically, the latter was the one emotional constant that surfaced in the 1999 LeoShe research. All moms were asked if there were things that they weren't doing a very good job on and which of those things were important to them.

One might think it would be things like cooking from scratch, keeping the house clean, and getting their families to eat more healthfully. But these were not even in their answers.

The answer across the board was what Fedewa calls the "motherhood gap." The things that mattered most to mothers were building close relationships with their children, expanding their children's horizons, and establishing the foundation for their children to live happy lives.

Companies today are recognizing mothers' desires to meet these goals in a better and more efficient manner. Let's look at Disney, the master of all marketers. Their position is that parents are expanding their kids' horizons by exposing them to the fun and magic of Disney World. Their marketing compounds that message by helping parents reflect on their own great memories at Disney World while they are appealing to the parents' desire to create those same good feelings for their child. All a parent has to do is sit along Main Street, USA, inside Disney World waiting for the electric light parade to start to get the message. I've never counted it but I assure you that the chorus, "Discover the Magic" plays at least a hundred times. By the time the parade has concluded, "Discover the Magic" has drowned out the theme song to "It's a Small World," which has been playing in your head ever since the magical boat ride hours before.

Pillsbury is another master at offering mothers a solution to the motherhood gap. Their tag line, "From my heart to yours," says it all. Pillsbury enables mothers to give a bit of what they remember as a child, baking with their mothers, to their children, hence enriching their children's lives.

Fedewa's favorite commercial, which depicts an example of raising a good person, a goal of all mothers, is a Hallmark commercial produced by her company, LeoBurnett. The ad shows a little boy who comes home from school. His mom finds a card that his teacher gave him in his backpack. Eventually she pulls out of him that he's been staying in at recess to play with a sick boy who can't go outside. It's done well because when the mother finds the card and asks the son what it is, he says nothing. She has to drag it out of him, just like you really have to with kids. She makes a big to-do about his demonstration of compassion and he responds with, "Mom, it's no big deal!"

"This commercial is a mother's dream. To have it so internalized in her kid that he didn't think he was doing anything special is a true sign of a success as a mother," comments Fedewa. "We showed the ad to our girlfriend groups and they all said, 'Yep, that's it. That is a successful mom.'"

■ ■ ■

We end this chapter the way we started it; recognizing that mothers come in many different shapes and sizes and with many different labels. Knowledge is gained in recognizing that it is not enough anymore for your target market to be "a mom." You have to recognize the diversity in the market and acknowledge your understanding that not all moms think alike. As a marketer, you must decide which particular moms are your market, walk in their shoes, view them as thinking and feeling beings, know where they are when you want them to hear your message, and somehow help them become better moms. Once you have applied these elements to your strategic marketing plan, you are ready to speak to them in a language they can understand.

## CHAPTER TWO

# Speaking a Language Mom Can Understand

Words often form the foundation of a relationship. Whether it's "I love you, mommy" or a simple "Hello," words set the stage for future interaction. The words you use determine whether there will be future dialogue with the other person. Speaking to mothers is no different. Advertising and marketing campaigns should be a part of a long, consistent dialogue with a potential customer and continue throughout the life of the customer. If we give credence to the hierarchy of effects (developed by Robert Lavidge and Gary Stiener in the early 1960s[1]), then we must believe in the importance of speaking with our customers.

## A Continuous Conversation: The Hierarchy of Effects

The theory of the hierarchy of effects is that prospective customers travel through six stages of a relationship with a product or service before actually purchasing it. In order to have the conversation result in sales, it must be lively, informative, and continuous. The six steps of the hierarchy are awareness, knowledge, liking, preference, conviction, and purchase. According to the theory, prospective customers are either unaware of your company or are in the early stages of awareness when you begin your advertising dialogue with them. If this is the case, you will devote a large part of your marketing budget to establishing credibility. If you are fighting for product preference, then much of your advertising must contain more competitive messages.

The amount of time it takes for the customer to travel through the stages can vary depending on your product or service. Lower priced products can take a customer up the ladder rapidly. Just think how quickly you travel from unaware to purchase when you are in the checkout line and suddenly make an impulse purchase. In a couple of minutes, marketers of the new widget hanging near the register can introduce you to their product, give you knowledge through packaging copy, and have you hand the product to the cashier.

## CUSTOMER RETENTION: AFTER THE SALE

By applying the stages of the hierarchy to a lifetime customer conversation, you will have the framework for developing a long and meaningful dialogue with your customer. I'd like to make an addition to the hierarchy, though. I'd like to add a seventh step: retention. The most meaningful and valuable conversation you can have with a customer is *after* the sale. Unfortunately, many CEOs and marketing executives have to be convinced to devote marketing budgets to the post-purchase customer. They hesitate because post-purchase customer marketing has a long-term return on investment rather than a short-term bottom-line impact. What they forget is that in just about every industry, it is cheaper to keep a customer than to obtain a new one. If I were saying this to a room full of marketing professionals and their bosses, every head in the room would be nodding in agreement. The problem is that few will invest in this piece of knowledge.

When I was in the car industry, it cost us approximately $360 per vehicle in marketing expenses to sell each car. That's $360 of margin that we gave away on each vehicle. I spent over a year researching vehicle-owner retention with my friends Pat LaPointe and Michael Charron at Frequency Marketing of Cincinnati, Ohio. Ultimately, we determined that you could retain a customer for less than $75 a year and obtain incremental service revenue in the process if you established customer loyalty to the dealership. In addition, a two-car family will purchase a new car on average every two and a half years. By focusing on retention, we were investing only $150 in our conversation with that customer before it was time for him or her to buy from us again. That's a savings of over $190 in marketing costs per vehicle—but best of all it meant almost $200 of additional margin. In an industry where a two percent margin is high, we were pleased with our loyalty platform. We even implemented a program that was on its way to hitting our projections. The customers loved it. The frontline salespeople loved it. So where is it today? It suffered the demise that so many good marketing programs experience when the folks at the top don't see immediate bottom-line impact. It was cut from the marketing budget before it could show meaningful results.

But the car industry isn't alone in ignoring the value of an existing customer. When I was in the newspaper business it cost $24 to acquire a new subscriber. The average price per subscription was $12. It was in our favor to retain our subscribers. Needless to say, the sales and marketing department had twice the headcount as the retention department because no one would commit to retaining old subscribers. What made the situation worse was that in the newspaper business you have an opportunity to speak to your customer every day through content and good delivery service.

My point is that once you get the conversation going with your customer, you need to continue the dialogue even after the sale. It is even more important in the mom market because mothers tend to be more loyal than men to companies they do business with, and, as we have already said, if moms like your business they will share it with other mothers. The remainder of this chapter will be devoted to the words and messages that connect, provoke, and drive mothers to your product. But remember your connection should not end with the sale. It is in the best interest of your company to keep a mom on your side as long as possible.

My grandmother Betsy used to say, "You never call," even if I had called only a few days earlier. Most mothers are just like my grandmother; they want to hear from you whether you are their shampoo company or lawn service. So speak to them and do it in words that are relevant and valuable to them.

## Starting the Conversation

How do you get the conversation started? Fortunately, this is not a blind date. You know important characteristics about your potential customer because you have identified your market and learned a little about her personality. You know that working moms seek balance and that June Cleaver: The Sequel has a different sense of self-actualization than a mother in an empty-nester life stage. You are lucky to know so much about the mom market. Now all you have to do is speak to her intelligently.

In order to make a proper introduction, focus on one of the core messages that speak to all mothers regardless of their parenting type, career commitment, or life stage. Among these are convenience, value, family health and safety, child enrichment, and balance. The last two elements have only emerged in recent years, which is an even further indication that the June Cleaver messages of the 1950s don't work with today's mothers. You can use any combination of these elements or one particular message to target multiple groups of mothers. (However, if you are advertising in targeted publications or sending a direct mail piece to a niche market, use the purest form and most direct definition of these elements that speaks to your particular market.)

Denise Fedewa of LeoBurnett agrees that it is okay to use a core message and address various subgroups of mothers. "It doesn't hurt a brand to sometimes be unspecific in their messaging to mothers. For instance, it is not necessary to define the family unit. There are lots of ways to talk to moms without knowing if they have a partner. Showing a real involved mom will click with several segments. You don't have to literally portray the client in the ad as long as it has relevance. For example, the Sizzle and Stir (2001) campaign shows Doctor Ruth and Mr. T as a family making dinner. The creator of the ad found an interesting way to talk about the convenience of their food. The core insight was universal because all mothers wish they had more family dinners," explains Fedewa. "The other thing this ad did well in speaking to mothers was it used humor. People forget that mothers have a sense of humor and they like to laugh."

## DELIVERING YOUR MESSAGE

The *delivery* of your message is what distinguishes it with your target market. The delivery of your message must have relevance to gain the reaction or attention of a busy mother. Your words will be wasted if a mother doesn't find them applicable to her life. It is for this reason that advertisers promote brands such as Sizzle and Stir with universal messages that appeal to multiple groups of mothers.

Kmart also does a good job speaking universally to mothers with the right type of messaging and humor. In the midst of its bankruptcy challenges, it has managed to produce some excellent mom marketing in its The Stuff of Life (2002) campaign. The television ad presents a parade of different types of parents in a common home setting representative of their market: a mother bathing children, a dad with a child in his arms, a mother with twins, and many others. Each parent says something simple about the realities of life as a parent, things any mother can relate to, such as, "Everybody has to buy a plunger sometime"; "You can't have too many juice boxes"; "They ought to sell socks and underwear by the pound"; and "Sleep past 7 A.M.?" Each ad ends with the Kmart logo and the tag line, "The Stuff of Life." These brilliant ads not only get you grinning but also tell you what Kmart sells: socks, plungers, and underwear. They speak to the core values of convenience and value. They relate convenience to the fact that everything from socks to plungers can be found in one place—Kmart. The ad speaks visually to value by positioning the parents in a modest home, which tells the viewer that all these items are affordable.

# Mom's Core Values

A FEW CORE values speak to the hearts, minds, and pocketbooks of mothers. These enable her to reach her goal—nurturing her children in the best, most efficient way possible.

## SAVING TIME (CONVENIENCE)

In the eyes of a mother, convenience is synonymous with saving time. Time, aside from the health of their children, is one of the most valued commodities in a mother's life. Time for her family, time for herself, time to work, time for her spouse, and time for the house are just a few of the demands on a mother's time. The one type of time we don't want to talk to moms about anymore is "quality time," a loosely defined term that carries almost no meaning to mothers today. The term was overused in the mid to late 1990s, and many mothers resent the term because it represents something not easily obtained and even less manageable.

Time is so precious that some mothers are willing to pay to gain a few seconds in their day. This is good for advertisers. Mothers' desire to find time can present a marketer with many communication channels. You can talk to mothers about how your product is going to give them more time, but another approach is to focus on what the mothers will do with the free time they gain by using your product.

PublixDirect, the home delivery division of Publix grocery stores, used a direct market message that talked about the time a person saved by using their service. Instead of doing as many advertisers do and using messages that spell out a specific use of time such as "spend more time with your children" or "take a long hot bath," PublixDirect simply said, "We can help you save time . . . how you spend it is up to you." This type of wording allows the reader to put her own value on the time she gains. Allowing a reader to assign the reward will translate into a higher perceived value than if you assigned it to her.

For instance, when I was in the travel industry and running a sweepstakes, I would much rather give away roundtrip tickets to anywhere in the United States than pick a destination to promote. Why? That woman in Iowa (or Los Angeles) who values a trip to her grandmother's house in Bismarck more than a trip to Las Vegas may be motivated to enter my sweepstakes if she has a chance to win tickets to grandma's. I might not even capture her attention if it's a trip to Las Vegas because she has no perceived value for that particular prize.

Another way to focus on the timesaving benefits of your product is to offer it as a solution to a relevant situation or universal challenge just as Sizzle and Stir did with cooking a family dinner.

For example, Tide provides timesaving tips, solutions for stains, and advice at Tide.com as well as an electronic newsletter written by Tide's Laundry Mom, Mary Larsen. The intent of the newsletter is to keep the conversation going with loyal Tide users. Tide marketers take it one step further by positioning a peer as the author of the timesaving tips. They are establishing the brand as not only a good product but also as a resource for timesaving help. In this way, Tide walks the talk of their old tag line, "Tide was designed with you in mind." Mothers can believe that Tide was designed with them in mind when they so clearly project the needs of their customer. According to Jupiter Media Metrix, Tide's Web site is appreciated by over 600,000 visitors each month.

Bisquick takes a similar approach. Their Web site, www .bettycrocker.com, offers mothers "impossibly easy pies, hearty main dishes, and fabulous family desserts." Through the use of content and information, Bisquick communicates that it delivers an easy solution and saves moms' time.

Dr. Gail Gross, early childhood development specialist, agrees that saving time is a powerful marketing message for mothers. "Saving time is a big thing. I know that I don't have time to be waiting. I want to be free and I don't want to be told what to buy. But if someone says, try this because it will save you time, I will. Mothers have so much on their plate. They want to be at home, in the office, and raising healthy children. Anything that can be precise and concise will have mothers reaching for it," says Gross.

## "It's a Bargain"

"Value" is a word that moms understand well, particularly as they try to manage their family's finances. Neil Closner of BabyUniverse, a baby product store, speaks to a mother's appreciation of value in the product descriptions on his site, www.babyuniverse.com. "The descriptions of our products are written by mothers who by nature tend to establish the value of a product. They might say things like, 'this is the best buy for your money when it comes to an umbrella stroller,' or 'don't waste your money on the deluxe models, your baby will only use this product for a short time.' Mothers don't necessarily want the cheapest product but they want to know that they are paying a competitive price and that the value comes in good customer service and an easy shopping experience as well."

### The Trouble with Discounts

Guard against capturing a mother's value-conscious attention through promotions and discounting. The airline industry does this. Instead of focusing on the experience of family traveling, airlines have resorted to deep discounts to get the business of mothers. Although no airlines target the mom market directly, some, such as Delta Express, Delta, and United Airlines, do offer promotions more appealing to mothers than to the mass market. These types of promotions are evident in the "Kids Fly Free" campaigns begun in early 2000.

According to Michael Henderson, president of Continental Airlines Vacations, this is simply a marketing ploy in an industry that does not particularly cater to families. "The reason that these kinds of promotions are associated with ski destinations," says Henderson, "is because the percentage of kids traveling to those destinations is low. The airlines can claim that kids fly free but such a small percentage of families will actually take advantage of the promotion, there is little cost involved for the airline. These promotions present the airlines with an awesome communication platform without hurting yield because families don't really fly to these destinations in great numbers."

Although discounting is an effective way to get a mother's attention, it creates challenges later for a brand that wants to convert the buyer into a loyal customer. The discounting strategy trains the consumer to expect discounts and never gives you the competitive advantage over other brands that are also discounting. It is a dangerous game and often discredits the value of the brand. I advise against using this type of communication alone with moms. Moms are savvy shoppers and will see through hollow discounts or shady promotions.

Terry Whaples, a mother herself and president of Holiday Inn Family Suites, agrees that mothers want more than just deep discounts. "Cheap is not the answer, but moms do want to get the best deal for their dollar whether it is shoes, a hotel, or a dress. We apply this to our hotel. We give moms value for what we have, but in addition our product is unique. It is what keeps our families coming back to us year after year. When a mom finds a place that meets her family's needs and makes everyone comfortable, they are happy and will come back. In fact, when we ask people to describe Holiday Inn Family Suites, 'comfortable' is the word most commonly used. It is the combination of value and comfort that speaks to our mothers."

## FAMILY HEALTH AND SAFETY

Health and family speak directly to all mothers as well. Volvo is perhaps the most notable communicator of safety when it comes to mothers. I don't know any mother that doesn't believe that Volvo makes a safe family vehicle because of the years of safety-themed advertising they have run. Even Brandi Chastain, scorer of the winning goal in the Women's World Cup, recognizes the safety quality of a Volvo. In an "Entertainment Tonight" interview she said that she'd like to be involved with Volvo because of the company's safety reputation among soccer moms.

A cord blood registry ad that ran in the February/March 2002 issue of *FitPregnancy* magazine spoke well to the importance a mom puts on the health of her family. The ad copy said, "What you wish for your baby: to have your husband's eyes, your head for math and most of all . . . good health." The ad spoke to the universal wishing that goes with being pregnant, but then it emphasized, "No matter how bad you want the baby to have your brains, nothing is as important as its health." This is a good example of talking to a mother in her own language at a time and place that is relevant to her.

According to Marilyn O'Brien of Marketing Moms, a company that generates insight-driven ideas to help companies build their brand equities and businesses, women want to know that companies sincerely care about their health and well being. They can do that by designing products that tell mothers that they understand and care about their needs. A smart brand manager can develop an idea, position the product, and supply products that are relevant to moms.

"Women can tell if a product was really designed with a woman in mind. Take for instance Viactiv, chewable sources of calcium for women, which just launched a chocolate version of their product. Now there is a company that understands what women want and like—chocolate. Other companies that have done a good job at designing products to a woman's needs are OB Tampon, Quaker Instant Oatmeal Nutrition for Women, and General Mills' Harmony Cereal," says O'Brien.

All the products that O'Brien describes create an opportunity for the brand to speak to a mother about the health and well being of her family. If a company goes to the effort and expense of producing a product designed to meet the health needs of a mother, they must promote that important difference. OB Tampons did a great job of this in their "for women by women" product launch. I had never heard so much about female gynecologists as I did when OB Tampons hit the drugstore shelf.

Debi Davis, founder and CEO of Fit America, a weight-loss and wellness company, and mother of two, knows first-hand the responsibility a mother feels for the health of her family.

"One of the concepts we developed within Fit America was the identification of family needs rather than simply appealing to an individual person. Since most women are seen as responsible for the family's dietary well being, they are the ones who usually do the grocery shopping, plan meals, etc. Statistics show that it is not unusual for a family with an overweight parent to also have at least one other overweight individual in the home—usually a child. It was for that reason that we developed a program that would also appeal to 'family weight management.' Understanding the pressure mom is under to 'take care of her family properly,' and recognizing that she may not have the nutritional background required to do that comfortably, we made it easy for her with simple eating guidelines and alternative food options that offer better nutritional value within a given food category," says Davis.

"I was extra sensitive to the fact that marketing to women who had a history of weight fluctuations was not necessarily the same strategy needed for those who gained weight due to pregnancy and who retained it after nursing. Running ads in parenting magazines or doing promotions in Mommy and Me classes was a better means for reaching this specific potential customer," continues Davis. "My 'new moms' appreciated the fact that I understood their personal challenges and didn't simply group them in with those other women who simply had eating problems. I think, universally, women want to feel good about themselves and the job they are doing with their family. Any product that offers value, quality, comfort, ease, and efficiency all help to make mom's job easier while making her look and feel like the super-women she would like (and probably tries) to be. Everyone wants to feel like they are on top of things and in control of their lives. Products that promote that feeling will do far better than those that don't."

Tyson Chicken often plays off many of the themes that Davis describes such as quality, ease, and health (serving a meal that is good for the family). A recent radio spot talks about the freshness of their poultry and ends with, "What your family deserves." This speaks to the mother who wants to provide her family with the absolute best poultry product. It also speaks to mothers who aspire to make more home-cooked dinners by saying your family deserves a nice oven-roasted chicken for dinner.

## CHILD ENRICHMENT

Child enrichment has replaced the yuppie trends of the late 1980s and early 1990s, when it was important to own a BMW and Rolex watch. Today, the children of this same generation have become the visual signs of success. This trend can be seen in the emergence of the overscheduled child who is chauffeured from tennis to piano and private schools that have newborns on waiting lists for admissions.

Messages that speak to mothers about bettering the lives of their children, enriching their experiences, and creating more intelligent students can be seen in print and electronic ads. The success of Baby Einstein videos was based on mothers seeking a way to better stimulate young, developing brains with music and exposure to the arts. The continued growth of Mommy and Me programs, after-school activities, organized athletic teams, and private school all speak to the mother's desire to give her child every advantage possible. Today's moms want their children to be smart and successful, but they also want them to be happy.

Stephanie Azzarone, president of Child's Play Communications (a marketing communications agency specializing in products and services targeted to kids, tweens, teens, and moms), agrees that creating a solution for a mother's desire to enrich her child's life is an effective message to today's mom market. "Regardless of the age of their children, the key message that influences moms is 'this is good for your child.' The two most impacting selling points are: This will keep your child safe/healthy and this will make him smart/ more successful. The effectiveness of the second message can be seen in the proliferation of educational toys and educational Web sites designed for kids. If mom buys a toy that's educational, she feels that she is doing something good for her child, and as a result she's more likely to do it."

Today mothers strive to help their child gain a sense of self-actualization rather than self-esteem as they did a few years ago. Dr. Gross says, "Moms used to clap and praise every small accomplishment, but today mothers are focusing on the center of the child in hopes of helping them learn who they are and the talents they possess and discover who they are in the process. Mothers believe the discovery of self will later give them the strength to ignore drugs and other peer pressure. The challenge for marketers and advertisers is defining what happiness means to mothers. What might be happiness to one mother might not mean happiness at all to another. Advertisers look for help in defining a mother's sense of happiness by recreating her own happy childhood in ads."

This is where nostalgic marketing emerges. Advertisers take mothers down memory lane in an attempt to help them relive childhood experiences that can be re-created for their own children. The message plays to a mother's desire to create cherished memories for her own children. Home Depot ran ads during the 2002 Winter Olympics that featured a father building a tree house for his daughter. The intent was to say Home Depot enables you to create memories for your family: It might be a tree house, but it could also be planting a garden together or setting up a birdhouse in the backyard.

A number of brands have recently joined the bandwagon of nostalgic marketing in order to appeal to mothers. For example, in the recent "More Ovaltine Please" ads, the message is the same as the one today's mothers saw when they were children. This reuse is effective because it allows mothers to relive their pleasant childhoods while providing a solution for getting their children to drink something nutritious.

## BALANCE AND SIMPLICITY

Balance has become an important touch point for mothers. The search for balance includes simplifying one's life, growing spiritually, and just feeling good. This trend is apparent in magazines, merchandising, and of course advertising. Most obviously you can see it in the popularity of the new magazine *Real Simple.* The desire to find balance can also be seen in the growing number of professionals who are foregoing their careers in order to work fewer hours and spend more time with their families. It was only a few years ago that Brenda Barnes, president and CEO of the hugely profitable Pepsi-Cola North America, left corporate America to spend more time with her family. Barnes is not alone. According to a study by the Radcliffe Public Policy Center, 61 percent of Americans would be willing to trade money for family time by giving up some of their pay for more time with their children or other family members.[2]

Balance is not a touch point isolated to working mothers. Balance can mean simplifying household areas in order to eliminate some of the time devoted to daily chores. Take a stroll down the aisles of your neighborhood Target store and you'll find hundreds of products devoted to the idea of simplifying. You'll see shelf, closet, and home office organizers, color-coded toy bins, and seasonal celebration kits complete with holiday plates, cups, and napkins. Everything in one store all with one mission: to make life easier.

Sears skillfully applied the "simplify" theme to a new line of mix and match children's clothing. Moms don't even have to figure out what top goes with which pair of shorts because Sears has done it for them. To continue their valuable conversation with their customers, Sears launched the KidVantage Club, a loyalty program that rewards mothers for buying their children's clothing at Sears. The program even offers mothers solutions for children who are hard on their blue jeans and tennis shoes. The KidVantage Club offers the Wear Out Warranty. If your kids' clothing or kids' shoes wear out before they're outgrown, Sears will replace them free in the same size.

Bruce Tait, of Fallon Brand Consulting, agrees that messages promising balance dominate the ad copy that connects with mothers today. "The big issue that seems to work these days is the idea of balance. Mothers have so many things pulling at them whether it's convenience versus quality or work versus family, that the idea of balancing life's challenges is important."

Tait decided to use the issue of balance while working with a beef company that was launching a line of precooked beef. Says Tait, "We wanted our marketing campaign to tell mothers, 'Here is a product that is pure meat, one not filled with chemicals. This product gives you the opportunity to serve your family a real roast and the best part is that it's easy.' Our precooked beef products were a solution for moms who were looking for the balance between life and the demands of a family. Our product allowed moms to bring the family together for a real meal," explains Tait. "It works well with multiple segments of mothers. For the traditionalist mother, it gives them the opportunity to serve a home-cooked meal with enough space to add their special touch. For the me-moms it gives them a convenient solution to serving a real roast in record time to their family. Either segment of mothers deal with the challenge of balance just a little differently."

Words can be combined with actions to create a marketing platform based on an experience. An example of this can be seen most obviously when an advertiser is short on creativity and produces an ad that simply asks the reader, "Remember where or how you felt the first time you tried <insert product name> here?" These copywriters would have been better off describing the smells, tastes, and scenes of the experience.

Some consumer product companies, however, such as Geneva cookies, are leveraging desirable experiences to a mother. Geneva uses humor and escapism. A recent radio spot depicts a woman describing the experience of eating a Geneva cookie. In great detail she describes every aspect of the cookie down to its crispness and finally you hear her yodeling in delight at the experience. The tag line is "Never have an ordinary day." It's an appealing message to a mother busy juggling work and family or a mother who is bored with daily chores. In either instance, it gives a mother imaginary solutions for escaping the daily grind.

## Quality Service

REGARDLESS OF THE product you are trying to market, providing excellent service is the most important element of creating a good consumer experience. Delivering superb service includes providing it before, after, and during the delivery of the product.

The number one reason that customers give for switching products or service providers is poor service. Quality service is even more important than price, location, convenience, and selection. No one appreciates good service more than a busy mom. For women who are already feeling the pinch on their time, good service can mean the difference of a few extra minutes in their day.

■ ■ ■

Ironically, as I was writing this chapter I took a break to flip through my mail. Within the pile of bills, magazines, and credit card offers was a direct mail piece from Charles

Schwab. Being immersed in the topic of marketing to moms, I took a moment to take a closer look and couldn't help but shake my head at the efforts of the marketer who mailed me such an irrelevant piece of mail. On the front cover was a picture of a professional looking African American man and inside a long, wordy explanation about what Charles Schwab could do if they were managing my 401K. Besides the fact that I do have a 401K account with another money manager, I was left wondering what relevance this marketing piece had to my life. It did not address even one core value of my life—not my roles as a mother, business owner, or professional. Other than my name and address on the letter compliments of a mail-merge program, the piece could have been mailed to just about anyone. It never spoke to me. Shame on the marketers who wasted their budget on advertising materials that didn't speak in a language that this mom could appreciate. Don't make the same mistake yourself.

## CHAPTER THREE

# Stay-at-Home Versus Working Moms

WORKING MOMS VERSUS stay-at-home moms—the battle lines have been drawn time after time in the media. Does a war exist? I'm asked this question frequently when interviewed on the topic of working moms. Often the question comes from radio producers and news reporters looking for a new twist on an old subject. Generally, the amount of energy expended in a typical "mom day," whether working outside or inside the home, is similar. Sure their sources of fatigue and stress may differ, but to label one role easier or harder than the other is foolhardy. A recent Dodge Caravan ad in *Yahoo! Life* says it best. The heading says, "What Idiot Coined the Phrase, 'Stay At Home Mom?'" The graphic is a picture of a mom with two children balancing a child on her lap and ice cream cones in her hands. In the background is a Dodge Caravan. The ad copy reads, "It's more like, 'pedal to the metal, go-go-go Mom.' And she drives a Caravan. . . . So, Mr. Catchphrase, stick your little label somewhere else." Well said. All moms work hard and are on the go, period.

I don't like to perpetuate the working versus stay-at-home argument. So why did I devote an entire chapter to this subject? Because it is the most recognizable point of division in the mom market, not only for the media but for so-called knowledgeable marketers as well. The working mom versus stay-at-home mother line has been the line of demarcation for advertisers who want to target specific groups of mothers. Ask an advertiser if he is going to target a particular group of mothers and nine out of ten times, he will say, "Yes, we are going to target working mothers"—as if the only two groups of mothers that exist are those that work and those that don't.

Let me fill you in on a little secret. If you segment mothers in this way, you will miss all moms by a mile. You will alienate the stay-at-home mother market by your lack of appreciation for the work that she does and you will miss out on the large part of the mom market that falls in between these two ends of the spectrum. You will miss the moms who work full-time at home thanks to telecommuting and those who job share. Mothers work today in a variety of ways and fashions.

As we learned earlier, mothers come in all shapes and sizes. In a similar way, mothers spend their day in a wide variety of ways, from being the CEO of a multimillion-dollar business to being the full-time CEO of their household. Today's mothers are creating a magnitude of new classifications within the working and non-working mother segments of yesteryear. The segment doesn't exist in the form that it did a decade ago. If you apply your marketing plan to images of the working versus non-working divide, you will fail. Just as June Cleaver has become a Sequel, working mothers have gone through a metamorphosis.

# A Brief History of the "Battle"

IT IS NOT entirely wrong to segment mothers as working outside versus inside the home as long as you fully understand the history, emotions, and ever-changing definitions. The core of the working versus stay-at-home argument lies in what our culture, communities, and individuals believe is the best situation for a child. As mothers began reentering the workforce in the late 1960s, a debate began to rage over the well-being and future development of babies raised in day care or by nannies while moms went off to pursue a career. I am not writing this book to support or discredit either side. I'll leave that to the hundreds of articles already written on the subject.

However, the constant media debate over whether it is acceptable to work or best to stay at home has created an unavoidable internal argument in the minds of many mothers. Combined with the natural desire to be a good mother, moms feel pressure when it comes to the work versus stay-at-home question. The influx of public opinion puts a great deal of pressure on new mothers to make the right decision for their child. In fact, from the time that the stick turns blue, everyone has an opinion about what is best for your baby and isn't afraid to share it with you. A new mother faces the dilemma of dividing her time, altering the identity she has developed professionally, and doing the right thing for her child. The struggle to do the right thing doesn't only involve making the right choice for her baby, but also includes grappling with the reality of a loss in personal income, the perceived demise of professional growth, and an adjustment in personal identity or lifestyle. The end result, regardless of the option she chooses, can be feelings of guilt, fear, or resentment.

All of these emotions can be present in various degrees of intensity throughout different stages of motherhood. It is important to recognize the range of emotions associated with a mother's decision to work inside or outside the home—most marketers assume the struggle only involves guilt. Think about how many ad campaigns you see offering a solution to the guilt associated with working.

The reality of the market is that guilt is not the only emotion associated with the working versus nonworking decision. Moms who decide to stay home go through a transition in their personal identity. Going from Jane Doe, teacher and wife, to Jane Doe, mother and wife, throws them off. Any change in a person's identity causes at least a short-term transition. Some mothers experience a smooth transition while others may experience strong resentment of their new role.

Marketing professionals must recognize the challenges of each segment of the mom market. Remember that identifying the distinct challenges of each mother is quite different from taking sides. You can target a segment, but always be careful of alienating another in the process. Since the battlefield tends to be more often than not an illusion of the press, I would caution any consumer product company or service provider in joining the army of one group or the other.

When we launched BlueSuitMom.com, we did so because I was a working executive mother myself and saw an untapped niche market with a need for information. The available parenting information was "generic." It was information I could get anywhere from anyone, but if I needed to find out how I could stay connected with my children while I was traveling four days a week on business, I couldn't find it. As an executive working mother, I had particular needs and I needed someone to speak to me in a language I could comprehend. I wanted someone to recognize me and understand my daily challenges. Yes, authors of working-mother articles could speak to the guilt I felt when I thought of my children 3,000 miles away with the chicken pox, but they didn't speak to my need as a woman struggling to maintain a strong identity in the corporate world.

# Why Mothers Work

MOST WORKING MOTHERS are created out of mothers attempting to fill two different needs. First are women who choose to continue working because they enjoy work and want to pursue a career. Second are moms who work because they have a need for the income to meet household expenses. In each group, some will be married but many will not be, particularly in the latter group. In fact, according to the Census Bureau, the fastest growing segment of the U.S. population is single mothers.[1]

Working mothers, with or without a spouse, number nearly 25.8 million.[2] Although recent trends show a slight decrease in the number of mothers returning to work after giving birth, two out of three mothers with children less than five years of age return to work, according to the same Census Bureau report.

The type and amount of work that working mothers perform varies as well. Many hold traditional nine-to-five jobs but more and more are taking advantage of the growing number of job options available to women with children.

Work options today include job sharing, part-time hours, flex schedules, and telecommuting. In addition, a record number of women are starting their own businesses. According to the Women's Center for Business Research, the number of women-owned firms increased at twice the rate of all firms between 1997 and 2002.[3] This is four times the rate of men who are becoming entrepreneurs. The sales from these businesses generate over $1.15 trillion.[4] Women are starting these businesses inside as well as outside their homes. In the United States, home-based women-owned businesses number 3.5 million and provide full- or part-time employment for an estimated 14 million people.[5] This option is particularly attractive for women with children because it allows them to be in the home with their children and earning income at the same time. It does, however, take a great deal of organization, motivation, and determination to succeed.

In my first book, *The Women's Home-Based Business Book of Answers* (Prima, 2001), I profiled forty women who had successfully built home-based businesses. Several women, such as Amilya Antonetti, founder of SoapWorks, and Julie Ainger-Clark, founder of Baby Einstein, have built multimillion-dollar businesses while balancing the demands of their children.

The life of a working mother is harried. She must maintain a household while being subjected to the demands of a job. Often there is little flexibility in work hours and even less predictability with their time. A child that is suddenly sick can create a major hiccup in the routine of a working mother. Working mothers are burdened with starting a second shift of work when they arrive home each evening. Before their day ends they must complete a long list of duties that includes cooking dinner, preparing for the next day, doing laundry, correcting homework, reviewing schoolwork, and paying bills. For those who are trying to run their own business, a third shift of work exists after the family goes to bed, when they can return e-mails, write business proposals, or fulfill orders well into the early hours of the morning. Working after midnight was one of the consistent traits of the women business owners I chronicled in my first book.

## Understanding Conflicting Emotions

IT IS IMPORTANT to recognize the emotions that working mothers experience while juggling the demands of their professional and personal life. Although most working mothers feel guilt or conflict at one time or the other, their feelings don't stop there. Working mothers love their children. It is just as important to working mothers as stay-at-home moms to be the best mother possible to their children. They have a deep commitment to their children's well-being, safety, and development. In addition, they have a desire for balance. Balance is the ability to feel fulfilled and satisfied in all the roles they play each day, and how this is achieved differs from individual to individual according to the amount of importance they give each of the elements in their life. For instance, a mother with a great sense of self-worth may only find a sense of balance when she is feeling fit and in shape. Another mother only feels like life is balanced if she is leaving the office every day in time to share dinner with her family. It is true, however, that many of the emotions a working mother feels are produced out of conflict.

Carol Evans, mother of two and CEO of Working Mother Media, agrees that working mothers live a harried life. "It's not just that these women are busy—all mothers are busy. And it is not just that they have a greater need for products and services that simplify their lives and save them time. It is essential to realize that working mothers want the whole experience of motherhood—the complex joy and strife, the deep emotional connection, and the funny, fun family stuff—at the same time that they are intending to excel at their jobs. These are smart capable people, and marketers must tap into them by recognizing their complexity, their capabilities, and their enormous desire to succeed in all aspects of their lives," explains Evans, whose company publishes *Working Mother* magazine.

Bonnie Ulman of The Haystack Group says that the emotional struggles working mothers face are presented on many different fronts—mom to mom, mom to herself, and mom to other people. Stay-at-home mothers who question the working mother's decision to leave their child with a nanny or day care may generate the mom-to-mom conflict. As a working mother, I can tell you that all it takes is for a stay-at-home mom to ask, "Aren't you worried that you're harming your children by taking them to day care?" to throw you into this internal boxing ring. On the other side of the fence, stay-at-home mothers can be thrown into feelings of purposelessness when the inevitable cocktail party question is thrown their way, "So what do you do for a living?" The mom-to-herself struggle can occur when a working mother sends store-bought cupcakes to her child's scout meeting rather than baking them herself as the other moms do. The mom-to-other-people conflict surfaces when a homeroom mother assumes that a working mother doesn't have the time

# Statistics on Working Mothers

HERE'S SOME HARD data that is beneficial to understanding the working mother segment:

- A 2001 Catalyst study of women born between 1964 and 1975 revealed that 68 percent said commitment to personal and family responsibilities is a barrier to women's advancement in their careers.[6]
- By 2005, the percentage of women in the labor force is projected to rise to 61.7 percent, while the number of men in the workforce will decline from 74.9 to 72.9 percent.[7]
- Nearly 70 percent of those who hold two or more part-time jobs are women.[8]
- Regardless of their employment status, almost nine in ten women—88 percent—agree that they are responsible for taking care of the people in their families, and 94 percent say that they feel very or somewhat valued by family and friends for fulfilling responsibilities at home.[9]
- Women who work full-time are more likely to feel more valued at home than those who work part-time or are at home full-time caring for their families (63 percent versus 56 and 57 percent, respectively).[10]
- Even if money were not a consideration, 48 percent would choose to work part-time or full-time. Thirty-one percent would choose to work at home caring for the family, and 20 percent would select volunteer work.[11]

to volunteer in the classroom, so she doesn't bother asking. The end result is the working mother feeling like an outsider in her children's school life.

# The Challenges of Stay-at-Home Moms

JUST AS THERE are many types of working mothers, stay-at-home moms come in different flavors as well. There are mothers who consider themselves stay-at-home moms who run home-based businesses, freelance a few days a month, or dabble in some type of income-earning venture. Many companies such as Avon, Amway, Mary Kay, and Melalucca have built successful sales organizations by attracting stay-at-home moms. Of course, there is also a large population of stay-at-home mothers who are 100 percent dedicated to the care of their home and family.

The day-to-day routine of a stay-at-home mom can be just as challenging as that of a working mother. They must manage the demands of a household while interacting with their children, sometimes nonstop, all day. They struggle constantly to keep their child entertained, engaged in activity, and out of harm's way. They share the long list of duties of a working mother when it comes to maintaining a handle on bills, homework, laundry, and cooking. Stay-at-home moms find other people aside from their own children pulling at their apron strings. A stay-at-home mom can find herself donating more volunteer hours to schools, PTAs, athletic organizations, and nonprofit groups than a full-time working mother devotes to being at the office. In addition, approximately 850,000 students were being homeschooled during the spring of 1999, with almost 90 percent of these children being taught by their mothers.[12]

The emotions of a stay-at-home mother are more than the nurturing joys of being there for her child's first step. Home for the betterment of her children, she experiences moments of loneliness and boredom. Particularly for women who maintained a strong identity outside of the home prior to having children, there can be a real sense of loss as they adjust to their new role as full-time mother. Others can impact their emotions about mothering as well. A stay-at-home mother can question the value others see in her work, even if she believes she is doing the best thing for her family by being in the home.

# Changing Roles

THE DECISION TO stay at home or work may change many times during the lifetime of a mother. The transition between roles often brings with it the challenges people experience with change. However, when a mother experiences change, the entire family feels the impact.

There is a growing group of rejoiners, mothers reentering the workforce after being home with a child. These mothers may rejoin the workforce because of a divorce or as a way to satisfy a personal need for professional growth or increased income. According to the Census Bureau, there are 7.6 million single, working mothers in the United States. Forty-one percent of them have never been married.[13]

Women reentering the workforce experience a great deal of anxiety. They are suddenly faced with balancing challenges they have never faced before. For those women who never worked outside the home while having children, there is the sudden realization that time is even more valuable and limited than it was while they were at home. For those who are married and returning to work, there is a necessary re-delegation of responsibilities that requires the entire family to take on new roles. Such a change can cause conflict in many different areas. A teenager might have to suddenly fix his own dinner or a husband might have to learn to do the laundry to facilitate the new household schedule.

A working mother who decides to leave the workplace to assume the role of a full-time mother can also be faced with new challenges. She must adapt to a new peer group and es-tablish new friendships and relationships. One of the com-ments I hear most often from mothers going through this transition is that it is difficult to make new friends. The chal-lenge is knowing where to go to find other mothers to social-ize with. This is where the local park begins to play its role as an important marketing tool. Just as we looked to the park to find mothers, mothers look to parks to market themselves. I always advise new stay-at-home moms to hang out at the park during the workweek.

The events of September 11, 2001, have motivated moms to rethink their priorities. Topping the list is a new sense of the importance of family. For mothers, this has meant a reevaluation of working outside the home or being away from their family for business purposes. It has also made mothers more committed than ever to finding solu-tions for work and life balance. In some families, recent events have meant unemployment, layoffs, or furloughed jobs for fathers, requiring stay-at-home mothers to rejoin the workforce to make up for lost family income.

■  ■  ■

So what do I say when asked about the alleged mommy wars? American mothers need to use their motherly intuition and do what they feel is best to meet the needs of their children, their partners, and most of all themselves. The good news is that more and more women are doing this. The ability and opportunity to make these decisions eliminates the old stereotypes of stay-at-home mom versus working mother. It's up to you as an advertiser to keep up with the changing roles of mothers. Your sales numbers depend on it because whether they are working outside or inside the home, mothers care about their children, themselves, and their households. The opportunity for savvy marketers is that moms will spend money to keep themselves and their families healthy, happy, and in balance.

## CHAPTER FOUR

# Using Radio, Television, and Print Advertising

T ALK ABOUT MARKETING to moms and the first thing that comes to mind is advertising. Advertising, particularly electronic advertising, reaches large audiences. Although it is not always segmented to reach your niche market, even untargeted ads can create brand awareness. A common mistake made by marketers is assuming that electronic advertising is too expensive, so they settle on other means of advertising, such as print. There is nothing wrong with print ads, but choosing a particular medium just because the price is right may be unwise. Clients tell me that they buy newspaper ads because they can afford them. They never even consider if their market actually reads that particular paper.

When we launched BlueSuitMom.com, our first instinct was to buy advertising in the *Wall Street Journal*. We wanted to target executive working mothers; executives read the *Wall Street Journal*, right? Then we took a closer look at their circulation data. To our disappointment, we wouldn't have reached our market. The media kit revealed to us that less than 50 percent of the *Wall Street Journal*'s circulation is female, and that small pool has even fewer women with children under eighteen at home. The numbers just didn't add up. Although I personally read the *Journal* every day, my ad would have been viewed by a lot of men, a few women, and even fewer mothers with children.

In this chapter we will explore advertising opportunities that effectively reach mothers and examine the advertising initiatives of companies who successfully sell to the mom market. By combining (1) the right message with (2) the right advertising vehicle targeted at (3) the right market segment, you, too, can create a successful advertising campaign. However, if any one of these three elements is missing, your ad will miss its mark.

Most industry professionals divide advertising into two categories: electronic and print. (The former includes radio, television, and online ads; however, we'll discuss online advertising later in chapters 5 and 6.)

## Electronic Advertising

BOTH RADIO AND television connect advertisers with large numbers of listeners and viewers, although television tends to be more expensive than radio.

### RADIO

We'll talk about radio first because, in my opinion, it's one of the best, untapped advertising frontiers when it comes to reaching mothers. It is particularly appealing for businesses with limited advertising dollars because it is affordable and reaches a large audience. The best part about radio is that moms like radio and have many hours of access to it. It is estimated that more than 60 percent of all radio listeners are female and over 50 percent of all listening takes place in a car.[1]

This is where you get to apply what you know about a mother's behavior to your advertising plan. A large part of a mother's week is spent shuttling her children to day care, school, and after-school activities or running errands in her car. According to the Surface Transportation Policy Project, a coalition of organizations interested in transportation policy, single mothers spend 75 minutes a day driving, while married women with children drive 66 minutes a day. Eight out of ten women (both working and non-working) are radio listeners.[2] The best part about the reach of radio is that a mom can listen to radio at work, in the car, at home, or at the park. Moms have access to radio virtually anywhere they go during the day.

Radio presents two marketing opportunities. First, radio provides basic spot advertising, which can be 15 to 60 seconds in length. Rates to advertise are based on the time slot and number of minutes you purchase. Every market is different, but radio airtime can run from $25 to $100 a minute in midsize markets. In addition there are also production fees. Most marketers include a catchy slogan, mention the company's name at least three times, and offer a bargain to the consumer they just can't wait to get.

Radio allows you to have a short lead time in your advertising message, which is perfect for special announcements. By including urgent marketing messages such as "limited time only," "act now," or "today only," you are able to see immediate results. Radio allows you to target groups of mothers with similar musical tastes or interests. When targeting to mothers, it is wise to select music genres that appeal to a conservative market, such as easy listening, Top 40, Christian, or country music. When buying radio ads, ask about value-added elements. Often radio stations will kick in tickets to local events, disc jockey appearances at your place of business, or concert tickets to use for customer promotions.

### Doing Your Own Programming: Brokered Time

With the many hours that moms spend in their cars, it is surprising that more radio executives have not turned their attention and programming to the interests of women, mothers in particular. Herein lies the second and most underused radio marketing opportunity: brokered time. Brokered time is blocks of airtime available for purchase from radio stations, which allows you the ability to air exclusive programming you've designed to reach your market. Brokered time allows marketers to produce their own programming. The growing popularity in talk radio makes specialized programming a new horizon for marketers who dare to be adventurous and creative.

My team at BSM Media applied these opportunities to create a unique radio-marketing vehicle for a client, the Chris Evert Children's Hospital at Broward General Medical Center in Fort Lauderdale, Florida. We assumed that mothers in South Florida were tired of listening to Brittany Spears and sports talk radio shows. Seeing the opportunity to reach moms while they were listening to the radio, we launched "Mom Talk Radio." The radio show is sponsored by the hospital. I host the one-hour weekly radio talk show, which features guest experts on a variety of parenting, balance, and timesaving topics. Since the hospital's goal was to reach all mothers, the topics are not targeted to specific subgroups. The show allows us to highlight the services of the hospital by including its physicians as guests and referring listeners to services at the hospital. What makes "Mom Talk Radio" successful as a marketing tool is that it positions the hospital as a trusted resource for mothers in the community. Week after week it is a place for mothers to turn for answers. When there is a need for family healthcare you can bet those mothers will be in the habit of turning to the Chris Evert Children's Hospital. It has been so successful that the original weekly show has been increased to twice a week.

In addition, the hospital has received the benefit of publicity by launching the first radio show for moms in South Florida. Their sponsorship of this show has resulted in newspaper articles in *South Florida Parenting* magazine, *Woman's Day*, the *Miami Herald*, and the *Sun-Sentinel*. We also use the show to announce other hospital events, thus saving the money it would cost to purchase radio ads. We have used advertising space on "Mom Talk Radio" to entice donors to the hospital's foundation. Donors receive 30-second spots in return for their donations. "Mom Talk Radio" was an out-of-the-box concept that has paid off in many ways for its sponsor.

Brokered time radio programming can help you carve out a niche and position yourself as an expert and resource in the eyes of your target market. There are easily enough niche programming ideas directed to women that you could have an entire network devoted to women's programming. Since mothers assume so many roles, programming directed at their roles will certainly attract attention.

## TELEVISION

Television advertising tends to be more expensive than radio because it reaches a broader audience. Just as in radio, production costs must be added to the cost of airtime. A more affordable option is to buy airtime on cable networks. In addition, cable networks offer a narrower market and may be more effective in reaching mothers. Networks such as the Discovery Channel, Oxygen, and Lifetime have made it easier for marketers to peel away layers of unwanted viewers. Ad representatives should be able to provide you with demographic and saturation numbers. Choose wisely before emptying your marketing budget on one national television ad, and if you do decide to spend it all in one place, plan well. Internet start-ups paid millions of dollars for a 30-second spot during the 2000 Super Bowl, hiring far-out advertising firms who produced far-out advertising that consumers couldn't understand. A year later, many were out of business.

The greatest challenge in successful television commercials is gaining the attention of your audience, speaking to them in a manner they can understand and with a message to which they can relate. Today's commercial viewer expects to be entertained. There is, however, a difference between entertaining your audience and going to such extremes that your advertising loses relevance to your target market. Many advertisers make this mistake. Not only do they give the company only a "by the way" mention, but the subject matter of the ad is so far removed from the value of the product that viewers become confused and disillusioned. Although it was not written to attract mothers, an example of this is a recent lawn mower commercial with big-breasted women mowing the grass and talking about the "power of the blades." I would assume that the ad was designed to capture the attention of its male-dominated market, but what do big-breasted women cutting grass have to do with the durability of the mower?

### Do Your Moms See Themselves in Your Ad?

A Kellogg's Rice Krispies ad, which ran a few years ago, is rerunning today in several markets. The ad depicts a mother in the kitchen reading a romance novel. From the other room, her child asks if she's done making their Rice Krispies treats. She quickly gets up, grabs the finished treats, and tosses some flour and water on her face in order to give her family the impression that she has been slaving in the kitchen when in fact she has been enjoying the time reading. The creators of the ad were appealing to time-starved mothers. The product benefit the ad speaks to is that Rice Krispies can be a solution for finding the time for yourself and still enable you to cook something special for the family. Where it fails is that few mothers who work outside the home can really picture themselves in the kitchen reading a romance novel, especially if they found themselves with a few extra minutes. These mothers would be using it to spend time with their children, or slipping away for a warm bath. Also, many mothers do not aspire to lie to their families. June Cleaver (the Sequel) mothers can, however, see themselves in the kitchen with flour on their face. In fact, they aspire to please their families in that manner. Kellogg's is offering them a faster, easier solution for obtaining their goal, leaving them a few minutes to devote to themselves.

Consistently across the market, mothers like to see themselves in advertising even if it is merely aspirational. Fortunately for marketers, mothers come in many different

# Finding the Right Logo

IN SOME CASES a logo can be the most important printed symbol of your company. The logo should tell the consumer something about your product or service. It should conjure up an immediate image for the consumer. A logo can also deliver a sense of credibility and public trust. In the mom market, trust is an important emotion to evoke, particularly as it relates to the safety and well-being of their children.

I find that in public speaking, people like this story. To find a name and logo for BlueSuitMom.com, I first focused on my target market: working executive mothers. I knew that the name and logo must contain the word "mother." On a piece of paper, I listed all the words that would describe my market: working, executive, mother, mom, business, and harried, busy, jugglers.

Second, I got out my crayons and a white piece of paper and drew a picture of my market. You don't have to be an artist to do this. In fact, you can start with a stick person. Include the tools they touch during the day, the people they interact with, what they are wearing, and a gender. My picture was of a woman carrying a baby on one hip, a bag of groceries on the other, a

shapes and sizes so your options are plentiful. With so many varieties of mothers to choose from, it is safe for advertisers to retire stale June-Cleaver type ads. Mothers today see themselves as the CEO of their household, whether they briefcase hanging on her shoulder. She was wearing blue pumps and a blue suit with a little spit-up on the lapel.

I kept that vision in my head for over a week, thinking of words to describe my executive mother. I substituted words for descriptions and pondered the question, "How do I put this visual into the heads of my market?" Then finally one day while on a training run for the New York City marathon, I came up with BlueSuitMom.com. The name puts a picture in the mind of anyone who reads it. A mom in a blue suit must be a working mother. The BlueSuitMom.com logo is simply the name of the company with a blue oval around the word "Mom." The oval was placed around the word "Mom" to highlight it because we felt that was the role most important to her.

We went through this same exercise to develop the name for our radio show "Mom Talk Radio." The message is clear: This is talk radio for moms. The logo is an easy-to-read font with radio headphones on the M of Mom. The symbolism lets the audience know it's a mom who has the earphones on at the studio.

choose to stay in the home full-time, pursue a career, or do a little of both. It is time to give them the originality in advertising that mothers have already created in their market. Marilyn O'Brien of Marketing Moms identified an ad that did a wonderful job depicting a mom in one of her twenty-first century roles. An Internet provider depicted a mother wearing bunny slippers at the computer, working from home while toys cluttered the floor around her.

"What the ad did well was portray this mother as clever and smart because she had found a way to work from home when she clearly had a child in her life," explains O'Brien. "For women struggling with work and family balance, the scene was the epitome of the advertiser understanding the need for creative solutions. The advertiser recognized these mothers need to be at home and use their brain."

### Tapping into Universal Messages

Denise Fedewa, of LeoBurnett, warns against creating ads that market to one group and turn off another. She says that it is possible to avoid doing so by integrating your advertising into a campaign that touches various segments with one consistent look-and-feel throughout the campaign. She uses Kraft as an example.

"Three years ago, Kraft did a series of ads in which they followed families around for days. They obtained clips of real families and highlighted segments of different family types," Fedewa explains. "There were inherently defined segments in families such as single moms with teens, African-American extended families with a well-defined matriarch, and a blended family with children from prior marriages. It worked because they recognized different segments within the larger market of families."

Not everyone has the advertising budget of Kraft. For those with a smaller marketing budget, Fedewa suggests selecting one segment of the larger group to feature in the ad while using a more universal message. You can cue into one group without alienating another. For instance, the focus of an ad for Hamburger Helper is that it provides working mothers with a quick dinner solution but the drama of making a fast and easy dinner is understood by the entire market of mothers. The entire audience sees and understands the message and figures that the mother in the ad just happens to be a working mother.

Many advertisers formulate campaigns around a common theme rather than segmenting the market. According to Bruce Tait of Fallon Brand Consulting, one brand that does this well is Campbell Soup. Their advertising campaigns play to the universal desire that mothers have of creating fond memories for the children.

"I think one of the most successful marketing campaigns targeting mothers came from a classic, Campbell Soup, when they brought back the Campbell Soup Kids in the late 1990s. The appeal of the ad was allowing mothers to reminisce about their own childhood while allowing them to provide the warmth and comfort of a good meal for their child. It is a good example of tying two strong messages together for the mother trying to create a nurturing environment," says Tait.

During the holiday season of 2001, Chex Cereal Mix did a similar ad campaign. They ran commercials that allowed a mother to reflect on the warm memories of her childhood and put the onus on her to make the magic happen for her children. It basically said, "Now you are a mom and it's up to you to create those memories for your child." It was strong because the ad connects a mother with her fondest memories and provides her with a solution to create them for her children.

**Capitalizing on the Desire to Create Happy Memories**
Bonnie Ulman, of The HayStack Group, who focuses on the
psychology of marketing, says that it is no coincidence that
companies are combining the nostalgia with the pursuit of
creating memories.

"Today's mothers love what tradition does for their family, and they are all about creating new memories for their
own immediate family," Ulman explains. "As her children
age, a mother will age along with them and along the way,
her definition of what makes memories will change."

According to Ulman, the critical instances or defining
moments experienced by a mother while she was growing
up set the stage for many of her behaviors and reactions as
an adult. These instances can be how her own mother par-
ented her or activities she experienced in childhood. Mothers draw on their own memories and apply them to their
style of parenting. These can be sensory memories as well as
visual or physical memories.

What forty-year-old mom doesn't think of red Life-
Savers or Vick's cough drops when they smell a deep scent
of wild cherry? I know I would be more likely to select
cherry Vick's cough drops over any other brand because it
conjures up visions of my grandmother giving me one out of
her purse. It's the reason that the Werther's Originals candy
ad with the grandfather sharing his Werther's with his grand-
son is so successful. It allows parents to relive a fond memory and create it again for their child. Ulman says that when
mothers view an ad like the Werther's ad, they are viewing it
both as an adult and a child. They are adults attending to the
needs of their children, but the memories of sucking on a
Werther's takes them back to childhood and how they inter-

acted with their own mother. Ulman says that the olfactory sense is one of the strongest senses. Hence the memories that can be generated by the smell of Toll House cookies, frying bacon, spearmint LifeSavers candy, and Dentyne gum.

The challenge for marketers is to find the positive memories without disenfranchising the mom. The flip side of allowing a mother to reminisce is that she has a natural desire to be the best mom possible, so the memories shouldn't make her feel like she doesn't compare to the mothers of yesteryear. The product has to enhance her ability to create memories for her child.

### The Rise of Occasion Branding

Experiences are playing another part in today's advertising. While some brands are taking mothers down memory lane, others are trying to create a place for themselves in mothers' daily routines. The trend is called occasion branding and is becoming increasingly popular due to the decrease in product brand loyalty.

Many things have contributed to the decrease in brand loyalty. Today consumers are influenced by deals, price reductions, or having different brand occasions. Bruce Tait describes the phenomenon of occasion branding, when consumers buy different brands in the same product category depending upon where they are at the time of consumption. He uses the example of a twenty-four-year-old beer drinker.

"Twenty years ago, if you were twenty-four years old you would drink Budweiser and that was it. Today, what you drink is a statement of who you are so you might drink different beers in different situations. You might drink one brand in a fancy nightclub, an inexpensive brand to keep in your refrigerator, and another at a neighborhood barbecue. Brands make different badge statements."

The trend of occasion brands occurs across categories. A mother's cleaning closet may include several types of detergents and various bathroom cleaners. A family's medicine cabinet will carry several types of toothpastes. Tremendous fragmenting going on today because there are numerous choices and consumers are taking advantage of them.

In order to capture consumer loyalty, many brands are marketing themselves for an occasion, according to Tait. "KitKat is a good example of this. Their recent campaign is 'KitKat: When you want a little break.' It is as simple as that. It doesn't mention the chocolate or crispy cookie. The message is when you want a break a KitKat bar is your best choice," says Tait.

The trend is taking place in the mom market as well. Pillsbury does a good job in their From My Heart to Yours ad campaign. The ads portray a mother baking with her children. The message clearly is that when it's time to create memories with your child, Pillsbury is the brand that takes the experience from the heart of the mother to the heart of the child. In print Pillsbury carries that image by adding a seasonal flavor to the kitchen scene throughout the year, in effect telling a mother that whether you are baking Christmas cookies or Valentine treats, the occasion of baking together should include Pillsbury.

# Print Advertising

PRINT ADVERTISING INCLUDES newspapers and magazines as well as a variety of smaller publications such as yellow pages, program ads, and point-of-purchase pieces. We are going to concentrate on newspapers and magazines in this chapter because we will be addressing other methods of printed advertising, including direct mail, in later chapters.

## NEWSPAPERS

Newspaper advertising can offer business owners many affordable options. Although newspaper readership continues to decline, for advertisers trying to reach more educated mothers with a higher income, it is a good option. When considering ad placement, it is important to recognize how a mother uses the newspaper. In addition to reading to keep up with the news, mothers use the paper to identify sales, compile their grocery list, plan their family's schedule with the event listings, and read the horoscopes. Believe it or not, the latter is one of the most-read sections by women in the newspaper.

Newspaper advertising is filled with choices, including the day of the week the ad will run, the size of the ad, color, and the section. The advertising representative should be able to describe the trends in readership and benefits of each product. Compare the information they provide with your marketing goals. It isn't wise to place an ad for baby products in the Sunday sports section.

Smaller local weeklies present a good marketing vehicle. Although they have lower circulation, the cost is more affordable. Mothers who read local papers to find service providers tend to be value-conscious consumers. Price and localized messages that picture the proprietor work best in attracting the attention of mothers browsing the ads in small neighborhood papers. The reader's perception is that companies who advertise in these papers tend to be smaller and aren't passing expensive marketing costs along to the consumer. Mothers are often attracted to small, family-owned businesses with the expectation that they will receive better service. This is where the natural tendency of a mother to want to better her child's community exhibits itself. Helping small businesses in their community is good for them and their children.

### What to Include in Your Newspaper Ad

Several important elements should be included in each newspaper ad whether you choose a full page or a one-column teaser ad. Every ad should include your company's name, logo, and location. It should also tell the reader how to contact you by phone or online. Give your customer as many ways as possible to reach you. This is particularly important for time-starved mothers. A busy mom doesn't have the time to figure out how to buy your product. You want to make it as convenient for her to buy your product as possible. Present her a compelling value proposition, one that will entice her to react to your offer. It might be a reduction in price, additional value, or a free item. Mothers are often the family bankers and, regardless of income level, money matters.

In all print advertising the use of white space is important. Don't clutter your ad with unnecessary copy or graphics. Keep it simple and easy to read. Your design and copy should take into consideration the lessons we've learned about the language and images that are relevant to your targeted group of moms.

## CASE STUDY: AUTONATION'S INNOVATIVE NEWSPAPER CAMPAIGN

The automotive industry has been slow to sway from the traditional price-point ads when it comes to attracting not only female purchasers but also consumers in general. Women make as high as 80 percent of the car-buying decisions in a household. In addition, the features that mothers hold important are different from that of fathers. Mothers focus on safety features such as automatic lights for times when they are in dark parking lots; dual self-closing doors on minivans for ease when loading children; dependability to alleviate the fear of being stranded on the side of the road; and storage capacity for balls, groceries, and backpacks. It is also clear that women do not like the car-buying process, which many find intimidating and often degrading.

Tom Gruber took these factors into consideration while chief marketing officer for AutoNation USA, the country's largest car retailer. AutoNation started out with a series of six full-page ads that were totally contrary to the way the industry ran ads. They spoke to customers in a way they had never been spoken to before by a "car dealer." The value proposition was a new car-buying experience. Included in that buying experience was a fully supervised play center for their child. Can you imagine the delight of a mother to know that she could spend time with a car salesperson without her children at her knees? It certainly wasn't the experience that she expected from a car dealer. That in itself was enough to get her attention.

"We sold image rather than the latest model of car or low money down. We sold the elements of our new car-buying concept. They included no hassle pricing, one low price, and great selection," explains Gruber.

One ad featured a couple enjoying a picnic with the image of a car in the foreground and another family having fun while washing a car. There were no prices in the ads, no payment plans, and no sale stickers. AutoNation was simply selling a

# Key Elements of Newspaper Advertising

- You have no more than ten seconds to capture a reader's attention and keep her from flipping the page.
- The message must be clear and instantly understood.
- The ad must sell a product's benefits rather than its features.
- Every ad should contain a call to action with some sense of urgency.
- The ad must contain contact information including phone number, address, and Web site URL.
- A good ad works like a salesperson.
- Ad copy should present a solution to a mother's problem.
- Design and copy must be in line with the product and company image.

new concept with a new way of advertising that spoke to all the things people hated about buying a car without actually spelling it out. Car buyers hate the haggling so AutoNation omitted the loss leader pricing and focused on the family scenes of mom, dad, and the kids enjoying their new vehicle.

The AutoNation print campaign followed many of the rules of successful print advertising. Good print advertising should be a part of a well thought-out campaign. It should first and foremost get attention. The attention value or device should be in terms of the product. Ultimately, advertising that does not relate to the value proposition of the product or service will fail. AutoNation's value to mothers in particular was that they did not have to spend their entire Saturday afternoon fighting with children as they tried to haggle with degrading car salesmen. The low-price promise meant there was value in the product and the large selection saved them time in the shopping process. Finally, the nontraditional ads were attention getting.

## MAGAZINE ADVERTISING

Although magazine advertising is far more expensive than newspaper advertising, it gives a marketer additional benefits. Women tend to save copies of their favorite magazines and refer back to them several months and even years after their publication date. In addition, they share their magazines with others, which means numerous readers see your ad, a fortunate phenomenon for companies targeting mothers. Magazines also allow you to reach a more targeted audience of readers, particularly if you decide to buy placements in a trade publication. Pricing for trade publications is in most cases less expensive and allows you to gain the panache of being a national magazine advertiser without spending the big bucks for a broader national title. Magazine advertising tends to be used more for branding than consumer announcements (such as sales and new store openings). In conjunction with publication dates, companies can design their ads to fit the seasonal needs of their consumers and capitalize on the magazine content. Magazines can provide you with an editorial calendar for their publication, a useful tool in determining the messaging and the focus of your ad as well as the best placement dates.

It's no accident that Children's Tylenol will run an ad in a special family health section of a magazine. Careful planning allows you to place advertising where and when it is relevant to consumers. Baking product brands take advantage of the seasonal calendar of magazines while keeping their messaging to moms constant throughout the year. For example, Duncan Hines will run ads that contain Easter-egg cake recipes in the March/April issues; in the fall the ad might include Halloween cupcakes. Both ads appeal to a mom's desire to create memories for their children in the kitchen but the subject of the ad changes with the season.

### The Four Essentials of Magazine Ad Design

Keep in mind four essentials when designing magazine ads: the visual, the headline, the copy, and the signature line. The visual should take up at least 50 percent of your ad space. Research indicates that 70 percent of people will only look at the visual in an ad. Realistic photographs work better than illustrations for attracting the eyes of mothers. As we have already discussed, moms relate best to ads that allow them to picture themselves in or represent a familiar scenario. If photography is unavailable, then illustrations are acceptable but they should be of good quality.

The next most-read part of a magazine ad is the headline. It is estimated that 30 percent of all readers will read a headline. It should be short. Here is your chance to evoke emotion and hook the attention of your audience. Apply the messaging and language lessons from earlier chapters of this book. Use a "to the point" headline that the market can relate to.

Your ad copy should support the headline with a compelling argument that supports the message of your ad. Again, keep this concise. Regardless of what segment of mothers you are targeting, moms don't have time to read lines and lines of ad copy. Ask most of them and they will tell you that they barely have time to read the magazine that contains your ad. Brevity sells. If you need a lot of copy to explain your message, then you haven't found the right universal message for your

## Creating Successful Magazine Advertising

- The ad must provoke emotion.
- The ad must contain a visually captivating graphic.
- The combination of copy and graphic must be intellectually stimulating.
- Copy must be brief, crisp, and concise.
- Message must be imaginative and engaging.
- The ad must differentiate the product or brand from all others in the category.
- Keep it simple.
- Include Web site, phone number, and other contact information.
- Identify your market and speak directly to them with a universal message.
- Don't be afraid of finding a balance between wit and wisdom.

audience and you haven't evoked immediate emotion for your product.

The signature line is where your company's name, contact information, and URL rest. Just as in newspaper advertising, give the consumer as many ways as possible to contact you. A complete signature line tells a mom that it is easy and convenient to do business with you; it's the first step to exhibiting good customer service.

■　■　■

Print and electronic advertising can be a powerful tool for attracting mothers. The right mixture of message, attention-grabbing graphics, and placement will allow a mother to see the need for your product in her life. Remember to respect her time, keep it short, and give her something she needs. Applying these concepts can mean the difference between generating sales and throwing your advertising budget down the drain.

## CHAPTER FIVE

# Developing an Effective Web Site Strategy

T HE INTERNET HAS been called the most revolution-
ary marketing tool of the twentieth century. However,
most marketers didn't expect mothers to emerge as one of
the largest group of active users. The early days of the Internet showed that white men ages eighteen to thirty-five were
the prominent audience, but according to Jupiter Media
Metrix, by January 2002, women had stolen the lead. The
good news for marketers is that women are not only using
the worldwide Web, they are spending money online. A
study released by Pew Internet and American Life Project
following the 2001 holiday season showed that of the 29 million American shoppers who bought gifts online during the
2001 holiday season, 58 percent were women.[1] The best part
is that with the right Web site, you can serve customers 24
hours a day, seven days a week. No wonder the Internet is a
marketer's dream.

Although early e-tailers got a lot of things wrong,
they were right about one thing—there is a lot of money to
be made online. There are now over 25 million women

online, according to Nielsen Media Research, and the number is rapidly growing.[2] More importantly to the topic of e-commerce, women are spending more online than men. According to Jupiter Media Metrix, in 2001 holiday spending women represented 53 percent of the $11.9 billion spent online. The most popular categories for female purchases include CDs, books, health and beauty aids, toys, and apparel for both herself and her children.

## Moms Like the Web

MOMS ARE NOT only surfing the Web and spending money; they are spending more time on the Internet than watching television. In a January 2001 study conducted by CyberDialogue, an overwhelming number of moms said the Internet is a great resource for finding answers to questions about kids and family. The same research showed that women, especially busy moms, are highly goal-oriented online, searching for quick answers and solutions. Eighty-eight percent of women rely on the Web for parental guidance and ideas, saying they are always looking for new activities they can do with their kids. Eighty-six percent said they made an online purchase, while 85 percent said they clicked on an online ad.[3]

When moms are online they often bring their children along. Eighty-four percent said they enjoy going online with their children, pointing to trusted family sites as the place to reach kids and parents alike.[4]

Diamonds may be a girl's best friend but the Internet might be a busy mom's best resource tool. Moms not only want technology in their lives, they see it as a tool to help them do a better job as a parent. When BizRate.com, a leading comparison shopping site, asked mothers what they wanted for Mother's Day 2001, 63 percent of moms still wanted jewelry and flowers, but technology gadgets ranked second on the list. In the same survey, 82 percent of moms said technology products will help them manage their family and balance their work and home lives.

It should come as no surprise that the Internet and mothers make great friends. There are literally thousands of ways the Internet can help a mother juggle the challenges of being a household CEO, business owner, wife, chauffeur, and parent. The Internet provides tools that serve many of the roles a mother plays in her family. If she is a pregnant mother looking for a name for her baby, she may let Stork Avenue.com, the largest printable birth announcement company in the United States, help her with its Find a Baby Name database; if she owns a home-based business, she can chat with other working mothers on Home-BasedWorking Moms.com or order her groceries at PublixDirect.com.

## MOMS ARE SEEKERS, NOT BROWSERS

If mothers face a challenge, they go to the Internet looking for a solution. It's that simple. Mothers tend to be seekers rather than browsers when it comes to their use of the Web. It's like the remote-control phenomenon. A woman will sit and watch a television show in its entirety while a man will flip from channel to channel catching bits of his favorite shows. A mother's time is sacred to her. If she wants to sit and be entertained, she'll find the show she wants and watch it. She doesn't have time for surfing, whether it's on the Web or on television. A mother will apply her tendency to be a seeker to finding information that she needs to make informed buying decisions or to obtain a solution to problems she is facing. Whether it is learning a cure for her child's nail biting or comparing credit card rates, a mother will go to the Internet and seek out what she needs.

Aside from tools to help with her busy routine as a mother, the Internet provides an important source of information. From the first time she hears the heartbeat of her unborn child, a mother-to-be wants information. Suddenly, there is a need for information on the latest health issues, stroller models, developmental details, popular booty colors, and nursery motifs. Whether it is her first or fifth pregnancy, the need to track the physical changes in her body and the growth of her unborn child becomes an immediate desire. According to online research conducted by StorkAvenue.com, expectant mothers search for baby names as early as three months into their pregnancy. What yesterday may have been a nonexistent concern suddenly becomes the focus of every waking hour. It is a joyous occasion, and if shared with the expectant mother can lead to strong brand loyalty.

Denise Fedewa of LeoBurnett refers to the environment that women have created on the Internet as "Hertopia." She cites several main functions that appeal to a woman's use of the Internet. "The heaviest use is for what I call 'my personal assistant'; this function attracts a lot of working mothers. They are using the Internet to be more efficient. Others use the Internet to find providers who will make life easier. Gift buying is a big convenience women also see in the Web," explains Fedewa. "Women don't necessarily need a huge selection when shopping online. They want you to have already done the work for them, that's why including features such as 'Top Ten Books' or 'Top Ten Destinations' works for women. You've already narrowed down the choices for them."

The Internet presents immense opportunities for marketers who want to reach the mom market. In this chapter we will focus on the strategies a company should apply in creating their Internet goals. Then, in chapter 6 we will talk about how we can use the Internet to gain traffic to our site and gather a large audience of mothers.

# Developing a Strategy

AS PART OF your marketing plan, you should have an Internet strategy. Five successful strategies have evolved out of the Internet rush of the 1990s. What we are speaking of here is Internet strategies used to support a business and not business models for online companies.

The five basic strategies for targeting mothers online are:

1. Information provider with no direct consumer sales.
2. Information provider with indirect consumer sales.
3. Sole e-commerce site selling directly to consumers.
4. E-commerce with integrated information.
5. Product information sites.

Let's look at some examples of Web sites in each category.

## INFORMATION PROVIDER WITH NO DIRECT SALES

An information provider can best be equated to an online magazine. The purpose is to simply deliver information to the consumer. The business behind this strategy might earn revenue from advertising, content licensing, or some other source. My own Web site, BlueSuitMom.com, falls into this category. BlueSuitMom.com is an online source of work- and family-balance information for executive working mothers and the companies who employ them. For the most part, we don't sell anything to our consumers but our advertisers find value in the large audience of working mothers we have built. They pay us for the opportunity to present their products and services to our audience. In addition, employers and other Web sites pay to license our content for use in newsletters, Intranet sites, and in other ways. Salon.com and iVillage.com are examples of this strategy.

Amazingmoms.com is another great content provider. Kit Bennett, founder and president of the site, describes it as offering solutions for busy parents who want to enjoy time with their children. Mothers can find articles that give them guidance on how to combine family fun with a busy day, have a stress-free party, and make easy crafts with kids. The content is updated regularly according to the season. For instance, Amazingmoms.com has articles on rainy day fun, summer vacation sanity tips, back-to-school hints, and holidays. Their free newsletter also provides quality content that parents can use with their children.

## INFORMATION PROVIDER WITH INDIRECT SALES

Muriel Siebert decided to use the Internet to become an information provider with indirect sales and brand building in mind. Instead of building a Web site that just sold financial services, Siebert acquired an existing women's financial site

and relaunched it as the Women's Financial Network, www
.wfn.com. The site offers women financial information on
running their businesses and managing their investments as
well as the tools to do so. The strategy works well because it establishes Siebert as a trusted source of information about
women and finances. It is highly likely that if a woman is turning to the Women's Financial Network to help her understand
the difference between an adjustable and fixed-rate mortgage
that she'll turn to the site again when it's time to invest her
money. Disney and Nestlé use the same strategy online, and
we'll look closer into how they execute it later in this chapter.

## SOLE E-COMMERCE

It's no secret that mothers like to shop so it makes sense that
some companies use the Internet solely to promote and sell
their products. Amazon.com, BabyUniverse.com, and Sure
Fit.com are just a few of the thousands of companies using the
Internet solely for e-commerce. The key to e-commerce when
you are targeting mothers is not only convenience but also intuition. Just as Denise Fedewa mentioned earlier, busy moms
appreciate it when you take a step or two out of the process for
them. It validates the "I'm saving time" emotion for mothers.
For example, Amazon.com does this by presenting other
books on a similar topic to the one you have ordered and
quick "peeks" into the first few pages of books of interest.

## E-COMMERCE WITH
## INTEGRATED INFORMATION

Some companies combine the two prior strategies by sur-
rounding their e-commerce initiative with useful information.

StorkAvenue.com has found a way to successfully execute this strategy. Stork Avenue is the largest printable birth announcement company in the country. StorkAvenue.com not only features their large selection of cards but also presents a baby-name database, safety information, and other valuable information for expectant mothers. The baby-name database in particular is an attractive tool for luring potential customers. It allows the mother to find a name for her baby and (how convenient) she just happens to be on a birth announcement site to help her announce the name of her new baby.

## Product Information

The final strategy is a straight product information site. Actually, very few businesses can use this type of site to the satisfaction of mothers. Most moms want more than an expanded nutritional label or online brochure from a Web site. This once was an acceptable strategy for travel destinations but today Internet users expect to be able to book a reservation or interact with you in some way while on your site. It's not enough just to provide a small bit of information to win over a customer online.

# Case Studies: Examples of Internet Strategies

## Disney's Internet Evolution

Marketers weren't always clear as to the direction to take on the Internet. Internet strategies have evolved over time. In the mid-1990s as companies rushed to gain a Web presence, they did so with little thought other than "We need an Internet site." Marketing strategists today can learn from the mistakes and progress of others without the expense that goes along with making mistakes. Let's look at one of America's biggest names in marketing and examine the evolution of Disney's Family.com and FamilyFun.com.

Family.com was launched in the mid 1990s as Disney's interactive way to connect with parents. The site is part of the Magic of Disney Online (www.disney.com), a division of Walt Disney Internet Group. The site offered content, fun ideas, activities, and interactive tools. By early 2001, Family .com turned its focus to a more specific target: the busy mom. They launched several new features and tools for busy moms and unveiled a redesigned site. Their strategy was to be a one-stop online solution center for busy women, especially those with children under twelve. The site spotlighted features and functions that attempt to make it easy and fast to find fun and practical solutions to life's everyday challenges. Their tag line was "Great ideas. Fun stuff to do." The site featured content, expert advice, community, and easy shortcuts to fun ideas. The site has solution areas such as Raising Kids, Parties, and Time for You to help moms better manage family life and find more quality time for themselves. Unique timesaving tools such as the "Picky Eater Problem Solver," enabled users to type in foods their child won't eat and receive healthful, kid-friendly recipes with alternative ingredients. To better utilize their other resources and do what Disney does best, cross-promote, Family.com partnered *Family Fun* magazine. The magazine became the exclusive content partner for Family.com. The partnership between the two media properties benefited mothers since it gave them access to shared content archives containing craft ideas, activities, recipes, vacation ideas, and updates on the latest events. Mothers love to compare notes. In addition Family.com included daily chats and message boards that allowed families to share advice and information on a number of topics including relations, childcare, pregnancy, health, and home issues. The content was compiled from dozens of topic-specific experts, including doctors, psychotherapists, and behavior specialists.

Family.com kept parents engaged with fun, interactive contests. For Valentine's Day 2001, they featured a "Keeping Love Alive" contest. Visitors were asked to enter the contest by visiting www.family.com and submitting a brief story of 150 words or less detailing the most romantic moment in their marriage since parenthood. In turn, they became eligible to win a grand prize trip to New York to see "The Lion King."

Eventually, Disney realized that running two Web sites could be three times the work without three times the benefits. One year later, in early 2002, Disney announced the full integration of Family.com with its estimated 1.1 million unique visitors a month into Familyfun.com. The revamped Family fun.com includes popular departments from Family.com. It offers *FamilyFun* advertisers special cross-promotional packages to run advertisements in the magazine and on the site. The change was part of Disney's attempt to develop the "Family Fun" concept across multiple platforms. *FamilyFun* claims to be the nation's largest magazine aimed at families with children ages three to twelve. It is also one of the nation's fastest growing, with a circulation increase of 100,000 each year since its launch. The magazine has a rate base of 1.5 million.

Familyfun.com covers family travel, learning projects, entertainment, and other family activities. Disney plans various promotional efforts to increase traffic, including marketing the Web site in *FamilyFun* magazine. In what is sure to propel consumer interest, Familyfun will be featured on the home page of flagship Disney.com. ABCFamily.com, the online home of the ABC Family channel, drives traffic to Family fun.com and includes content from that site as well. Adding Familyfun.com content transformed ABCFamily.com from primarily a promotional platform to a family destination site. In television support, ABC Family ran 30-second spots to announce Familyfun.com's new site.

## NESTLÉ'S ONLINE ADVENTURE

Other big name brands have staggered between Internet strategies before discovering online success. Nestlé began its Web site adventure with the intent of being a product information site. After fumbling through a variety of Internet strategies in the mid 1990s, it decided to become a resource for its consumers and ultimately evolved as an information provider with indirect consumer sales and branding. Once Nestlé discovered that the latter strategy worked best for connecting their brands to mothers, they found lots of way to integrate the strategy into their brand product Web sites.

By acquiring already established Web sites that contained content and an audience of their potential customers, they transformed their brand information sites into ones that customers valued. In 2001, Nestlé acquired Meals.com, which had emerged as a trusted site for ample recipes for just about any occasion. Meals.com has built a database of thousands of recipes and ingredients so that a busy cook can search by ingredient, ethnic variety, time restraints, or meal course. Moms love the site because it helps them manage meal planning.

In fact, when we launched BlueSuitMom.com, we quickly formed a partnership with Meals.com. We knew that 60 percent of working mothers do not know at 4 P.M. what they are going to serve for dinner and that to serve our customers we had to help them with their meal planning. Through the partnership, our mothers could search through the databases of Meals.com, which appeared as co-branded pages, while obtaining work and family balance information on other BlueSuitMom.com channels. Examining our Web logs, we found that almost one-third of our page views could be attributed to recipe searches. We applaud Nestlé for making such a smart move in acquiring Meals.com.

Today Meals.com has been reinvented as VeryBest Meals.com. It is the same great recipe site but now carries the branding of Nestlé products such as Ortega, Nesquik, and Juicy Juice. If I'm searching for a recipe for tacos, I'm more likely to remember the Ortega brand when I go to the store because of the Ortega presence on VeryBestMeals.com.

Acquiring Meals.com isn't the only thing Nestlé has done well on the Web. Nestlé's Web strategy now focuses on creating sites that help and inform consumers. Each of their sites carries the ubiquitous "very best" slogan. In addition to VeryBest Meals.com, Nestlé now has VeryBestKids.com, VeryBest Baking.com, VeryBestPet.com, and VeryBestBaby.com.

Moms who visit VeryBestBaby.com can find helpful information about recovering after birth, what it means to be a mother, health advice, a weight tracker, and even breastfeeding tips. As unlikely as it seems from a company that wants to sell moms Carnation baby formula, it works. The strategy gives Nestlé the most valuable opportunity in marketing—the chance to develop an interactive and loyal relationship with their customers. It allows them to develop credibility and trust, an emotional tie difficult to create through stagnant advertisements.

The presentation of multi-topic content on a Web site also creates an opportunity to introduce new customers to your product. Had Nestlé kept with their original Internet strategy, CarnationMilk.com, they would not benefit from traffic generated from search engines. Now, if an expectant mother enters "breastfeeding" into a search engine such as Yahoo! or Google, she will be directed to VeryBestBaby.com because the topic of breastfeeding appears on that site.

## Web Site Elements That Attract Moms

Recipes
Horoscopes
Salary comparisons
Baby name guides
Gift suggestions
Message boards
Chat rooms

Expert questions and
   answers
Databases of definitions
Ideas for activities to do
   with their children
Medical explanations
Vacation planning tools
Checklists

Limiting yourself to product information on the Internet limits your appeal to a broader market of moms as well.

# Reexamining the Role of Information Provider

LET'S REEXAMINE THE choice of being solely an information provider. This strategy works only if you are providing solutions or targeting a niche group of mothers. Moms do not have time to leisurely surf the Internet. They will, however, take the time to read content that presents answers to some of their most challenging situations. Your challenge lies in the execution of delivering valuable content to your market. You must have a clear definition of your mothers and what their needs are. As we have already discussed, not all moms give the same value to the same product, content, or advice.

When we launched BlueSuitMom.com, we were clear that our market was executive working mothers. We focused our content, story ideas, interactive tools, and presentation to this market. We even used tones of blue because we felt the color reminded our moms of their professional careers. Remember when designing your content-based site that there are literally millions of pages for your audience to choose from on the Internet. Your content must stand apart, either in context or quality. On BlueSuitMom.com we focus on both. Fortunately, my partner, Rachael Bender, and I have high editorial standards. The combination of quality content and unique targeted stories quickly set us apart with our audience.

For example, a baby product company deciding to be a content site for new moms will find the Internet playing field to be very crowded and will have a difficult time distinguishing itself. Just how many ways can you talk about the difference between disposable diapers and cloth? Find a unique spin to make a mark in the market. Well-designed, content-based sites that focus on educating on one particular issue of parenthood—such as discipline, ADHD, or colic—or join a group of mothers with a common denominator like adoption or infertility can be very successful.

## Remembering the Basics

WHEN THE GOLD rush of the Internet began, entrepreneurs clamored to the Web to sell their widgets to the millions of consumers suddenly at the door of their virtual storefront. They built their site, acquired a merchant account, put out their "open for business" sign, and sat back to wait for their millions to come rolling in. A short time later many found themselves wondering where the customers had flocked and why their operating expenses far exceeded their sales. What most forgot were the basic principles of retailing: customer service, selection, presentation, and brand trust. In many cases, it wasn't even forgetfulness; most e-tailers had never been retailers offline. In the frenzy of getting online and the promise of getting rich quick, entrepreneurs made decisions without much thought.

These new Web-based business owners were in good company; large successful brick-and-mortar retailers also made plenty of mistakes taking their products to the Internet. I remember in particular sitting at my computer wondering how one furniture retailer planned to ship a full-size bedroom set to online consumers, but, more important, who would buy $10,000 worth of furniture without jumping on the mattress or looking into the drawers. When building an e-commerce site for mothers, remember they are busy people. They want to simplify their life, save time, and work more efficiently. They appreciate doing business with companies who relate to their needs. In addition, when it comes to online purchases, they want to have a heightened level of trust in doing business with you. Trust, in fact, is the most important issue to address if you want to capture a mother's online purchases.

## Establishing Trust Online

IN VIRTUALLY EVERY survey of women and online purchasing, when women are asked why they don't purchase online, fear of credit card security is the most common response. Their concerns relate to personal privacy, lack of Internet regulation, stolen credit card numbers, and other transactions. In a 2000 survey by CyberDialogue, 40 percent said they are concerned about the security of the information they give on sites.[5] The lack of trust in your security measures can translate to the loss of big bucks. The same study pointed out that women who felt safe spending online spent an average of $830 compared to $459 spent by doubting females. Your first priority in designing your e-commerce site should be to establish trust in your potential customers.

My advice is that you cannot incorporate too many ways of telling your customer that it is safe to do business with you. Your first step should be to clearly display your privacy policy on the homepage of your site. Rachael Bender of BSM Media offers this guidance:

"Mothers look for a couple of items to know that a site is reputable. Does it list their address and 1-800 phone number? Does it have secure transaction through SSL? Most Web-savvy consumers know to look for the secure sign as shown by a lock in the lower corner of a Web browser. Does it have a privacy policy? Does it offer a return and satisfaction-guaranteed policy? In addition, you should obtain a seal of approval from the Better Business Bureau Online or Verisign. The Internet can often be a faceless entity. Mothers need to know that they aren't giving their credit card number to some guy working out of his garage and stealing credit card numbers," says Bender.

The American Marketing Association has a code of ethics for marketing and Internet that establishes guidelines for marketing professionals. Let's review three areas important to mothers—privacy, ownership, and access.

## PRIVACY

Information collected from customers should be confidential and used only for expressed purposes. All data, especially confidential customer data, should be safeguarded against unauthorized access. The expressed wishes of others should be respected with regard to the receipt of unsolicited e-mail messages.

## OWNERSHIP

Information obtained from Internet sources should be properly authorized and documented. Information ownership should be safeguarded and respected. Marketers should respect integrity and ownership of computer and network systems.

## ACCESS

Marketers should treat access to accounts, passwords, and other information as confidential, and only examine or disclose content when authorized by the responsible party. The integrity of others' information systems should be respected with regard to placement of information, advertising, or messages.

Kevin Colleran, president of PhotoMasterpieces.com (an online service that turns photographs into poster-sized canvas oil paintings), suggests that you confront a woman's insecurities by addressing them in the design of your Web site. "We try to anticipate questions and post the answers to commonly asked questions. We clearly list the address and phone number on each page, which makes our customers feel comfortable knowing that real people are behind the scene. This is important because of the bad reputation many Internet companies have earned. Shoppers feel more comfortable when they can speak to a live voice. In addition to having all transactions on a secure page, we include shipping in the cost, so there are no hidden extras, and offer them alternative purchase methods, such as PayPal. Our customers also like our confirmation page, which they can print out with all the details of their order. Each confirmation has our 100 percent satisfaction guarantee on it."

# Displaying Your Wares Online

ONCE YOU HAVE made your mom comfortable about buying from you online, it's time to show her your wares. Let's start with the presentation of your product. An e-commerce site should be clean, uncluttered, and have merchandise organized in a manner that makes sense to the consumer. Randomly placing shirts among coats and hats will only frustrate. Introduce your product to the consumer in categories. Categories can break out according to brand or by consumer use. For example, an online clothier may group all its Levi jeans together or group them in a casual wear category. Use good quality pictures of the products. If your technology budget allows, give the viewer the option to enlarge the photo or look at the product from multiple angles.

Many successful retailers also include product descriptions and customer reviews. These elements can help establish the trust of moms, who want to know that they are getting the very best product to meet their family's needs. The combination of buyer information and easy-to-find product presentation is particularly important for e-tailers with big selections for mothers. Neil Closner of BabyUniverse.com describes the challenge of finding the right balance between information and putting the product in front of shoppers.

"It is important to replace as much of the in-store shopping experience as possible. In a store, you can ask a salesperson to guide you to the product. Online, though, we can provide an even better experience by being convenient and informative. Unlike a brick-and-mortar retailer, we have the opportunity to have virtual salespeople who do have all the answers by offering consumer product information and buying guides, unlike in a store where there is a 50/50 chance that you will get a salesperson who really knows what they are talking about," Closner explains.

Closner explains that buying guides on his site describe what to look for in buying a crib or a stroller. His guides start off with a general topic, such as strollers, and then narrow down to information on niche products such as twin strollers or joggers. The guides keep in mind that many of his mothers have never bought a stroller, crib, or baby monitor before. The guides are strictly designed as a service to moms shopping on BabyUniverse.com and do not push high-margin items or preferred vendors. This useful information keeps them on BabyUniverse.com and is the first step in developing a relationship with the customer. Closner believes in giving a mother as much information as possible. Almost all of his information descriptions are written by mothers who have used the product themselves.

BabyUniverse.com organizes its merchandise by categories according to either product use or product type. Categories include bathing, feeding, furniture, strollers, and car seats.

"We used to have strollers and car seats together in a travel category but there were just too many products for our customers to view so we broke out strollers into their own category. You have to remember that mothers are coming to your site for convenience and if they have to search and search for the product they need, they will go somewhere else to buy it," comments Closner.

To ensure that customers can find what they need quickly, BabyUniverse.com has a prominently displayed Search tool. Customers can search by brand, product type, price, age-appropriate, and product name. The central navigation also contains the most popular search phrases such as cribs, high chairs, and play yards. This is BabyUniverse.com's way of doing some of the work for their mothers, something that we know moms appreciate.

BabyUniverse.com has added customer ratings to their product displays. This interactive element was made popular by Amazon.com and offers benefits not only to the customer but to marketers as well. First, allowing customers to talk to each other even if it is only to give their opinions on a product gets them interacting with your brand. If they get used to talking to you, they will tell you more of what you want to know, whether that is personal demographic information or what they like and don't like about your company or competitors. If they will talk to you about your products they are more likely to talk to others about them, too. Getting your customer into a dialogue with you is a very good thing.

General Mills, for example, engaged their customers by asking them to create their own cereals on MyCereal.com. Consumers not only enjoy creating their own cereals but General Mills is collecting thousands of pieces of data about consumer desires and attitudes toward cereal products. All of this is valuable information for marketers and is a perceived value to the customer.

## Simplifying the Buying Process

ONCE A CUSTOMER has selected a product to purchase, make the buying process as simple as possible. Amazon.com has mastered this skill, making it almost too easy for consumers to purchase with their three-step shopping-cart process. But most companies don't have the money to invest in personalized shopping technology, so we'll concentrate on the things we can actually execute on our Web sites.

Bob Hunter of StorkAvenue.com believes intuition is the most important element to a good buying experience for his expectant and new mothers.

"An e-commerce Web site should be an intelligent cash register. It should be intuitive to the customer's needs and recognize what the customer wants while making it easy for them to buy the product," explains Hunter, whose online sales now account for over 40 percent of his annual sales. "If you ask the right questions you can lead the consumer to the sale. They will make an informed decision and feel good about their purchase."

When appropriate, StorkAvenue.com suggests complimentary items to go along with the items that are ordered. For instance, if a new mother is ordering birth announcements, the shopping cart technology might suggest matching note cards or colored pens for addressing the envelopes. This takes the work out of remembering for new mothers who are sleep deprived and overwhelmed. Each order is followed by a confirmation e-mail, shipping message, and thank-you note. These elements are not only part of the check-out process but also represent another key component to executing a successful e-commerce strategy—customer service.

## Superior Customer Service

THE EXPERIENCE THAT a mother has with the purchasing process of your product can be the difference in making the sale or losing it. A company can invest thousands of dollars in advertising, but their efforts ultimately will fail due to their lack of commitment to customer service. Some companies have realized the importance customer service plays in earning and maintaining the purchasing power of mothers and have initiated policies to ensure the highest forms of good customer service.

Both StorkAvenue.com and BabyUniverse.com maintain their own offline customer service representatives to answer phone calls, emails, and faxes.

"Our mothers know that they can pick up the phone and find a caring person on the other end who will walk them through our birth announcement designs or check on their order. It is not uncommon for us to call a mother to double-check on a spelling of a name or color selection. We are announcing their baby to the world for them and it is a very special occasion. We genuinely share in the excitement of their new baby. It means a great deal to a mother when you care," says Hunter.

Closner of BabyUniverse.com believes that customer service is what separates successful online e-tailers from the others. There are many places on the Web for mothers to buy strollers and cribs, and Closner attributes his success to the high customer service standards BabyUniverse.com set from the very first day of operation. Closner prides himself on the fact that mothers can reach his customer service representatives without navigating through several telephone prompts. His customer service representatives are a team predominantly comprised of women, including many mothers. They are not only eager to help customers but often have personal experience with the product and can make recommendations or give firsthand advice.

# Where to Position Your Product

ALTHOUGH BABYUNIVERSE.COM AND StorkAvenue.com share many of the same good online practices, the two made different choices when it came to expanding their content beyond product information. The decision to remain a pure e-commerce site or to offer content as well depends largely on your playing field, your position, and how much content you actually want to provide. The team at BabyUniverse.com made a conscious decision early on not to try to be the leading parenting portal as well as the leading online baby product retailer. Closner recognized that there were more than enough players on that field and he wanted to focus his efforts on selling product. Instead of providing content to his audience, he partnered with content providers for newsletter articles and posted links to resources of interest to his moms.

StorkAvenue.com, on the other hand, has selectively integrated content that focuses on the safety of babies. Moms can find safety product recalls and articles on choosing a name for baby.

As another example, the Holiday Inn Family Suites site (hifamilysuites.com) was designed to be not only a booking engine for hotel stays but also an informational source for moms planning their family vacations. The site includes pictures of rooms, restaurant information, tours of facilities, entertainment schedules, and directions.

"Over and over again, we see that the most read page on our site is the page which lists food prices for our restaurants," says Terry Whaples, president of Holiday Inn Family Suites. "Moms want to know what it's going to cost to feed their family once they get to where they are going. We take one more uncertainty out of the travel experience for the mom. I think down the line, she appreciates that."

Whaples must be doing something right. The Family Suites Web site books more rooms than any other Holiday Inn property online. Whaples emphasizes the importance of pictures on a Web site, particularly when it is intended to sell travel. Whaples's Web site offers lots of pictures, including

360-degree tours, which allow moms to see exactly what they're buying in terms of a family vacation.

# Web Design Basics

SURF THE INTERNET for an hour and you are certain to find that Web designs are as varied as colors in a rainbow. Unlike printed means of advertising, such as newspaper ads or company brochures, your marketing decisions go beyond color and layout. The same interactive component that makes the Internet such a remarkable marketing tool also creates many choices for designers. Designing a successful Web site includes constructing customer-friendly navigation, writing meaningful content, integrating online tools, and installing software to support your online goals. Compounding the challenge is the lack of history to base your decision on. However, several lessons have emerged from the short history of the Internet that can contribute to a successful Web site design.

## DON'T OVERLOAD YOUR SITE

Be careful when filling a Web site with numerous photos. With each photo, you add load time to your site. A site with only a few pictures loads in about 15 to 30 seconds. Loading down the site with too many photos can delay your site from reaching your potential customer for another minute to a minute and a half. How can a minute mean so much to a consumer? When you consider the millions of sites waiting to almost instantly appear on your customers' computer screen, you don't want them to get bored waiting for your site to load. Internet consumers have been spoiled by the speed at which they can find information. If they cannot get it quickly from you, they can go somewhere else to find it.

My business partner, Rachael Bender, also warns against using flash technology, the moving and splashy images that create a rich multimedia experience for the viewer. Most consumers recognize it as the 'skip intro' feature on some sites. Although many Web designers use flash to give their site a state-of-the-art appearance, it can eliminate customers. A busy mother seeking information doesn't have the time to watch a flashy mini-movie before getting to the navigation of the site. Another problem with flash is that it requires the viewer to have the macromedia player installed on the computer. Although many new computers come with the program already loaded, there are a small percentage of users who will either not take the time to download the software or who will never be able to view it because of the age of their computer or their lack of computer skills. Unless you have a specific need and the research to support it, I recommend letting your customers spend their time on your site rather than with your introduction.

## EYE APPEAL

Just a few pieces of know-how can go a long way in selecting a design that attracts and serves mothers well. Your design should apply many of the elements we have discussed in creating advertising. The language of your copy and crispness of your graphics should be combined with appealing colors and easy navigation to create a site that quickly gets a mother's attention and helps her connect to the relevance of your content or product.

You have a rainbow of colors to select from and they can add more impact than you might guess. Just think what the color green has done for Heinz. Since they turned their ketchup green, sales have increased by $23 million. No wonder they are now introducing purple and blue ketchup.

However, I guard my clients against going palette-happy. Too many colors on a computer screen will confuse the viewer. I once heard a site that had too many vibrant colors in its design described as looking like a butchered clown. It's fun to play with colors but not at the expense of losing your audience. Colors can provoke emotional reactions online just as they do offline.

Dr. Gross, child development specialist, explains that people have unconscious reactions to colors. "Women in particular internalize things so colors will remind them of the environment around them and provoke the emotions associated with the connection. Green, for instance, represents money and the feelings that go along with it. That is why you will see banks and financial institutions using shades of green in their logos and advertising. Blue is a healing color. You will find a lot of healthcare providers represented by various shades of blue. With women, you have to also be aware that the taste for colors will change with their stages in life. Pastels are appealing for a new mother but not so for an empty nester."

Your market may have color expectations that establish credibility for your Web site. BabyUniverse.com, for example, uses the soft pastels you would expect to find when looking at a company that represents baby products. The consumer would be confused and possibly offended if she found a Web site designed in black and brown at Baby Universe.com.

In addition to color selection, clear navigation is extremely important to the design of your site. The use of a side rail to call out important categories of information is an easy way to direct your audience to the most desired destinations within your site. Topic navigation can be used to personalize the experience of the audience by directing readers with a common purpose to pages that serve their needs.

For example, a site we designed for Holy Cross Hospital in Fort Lauderdale Hospital has top navigation that directs visitors, patients, and health care professionals to different areas of the site, which contain information customized to their role within the hospital. Patient information has particulars on admitting and insurance while the Professional area contains employee information. Since the experience of visiting the site is different for each group, it makes sense to direct them down the shortest path. The better the experience for consumers, the more likely they are to return. It's not much different from brick-and-mortar destinations.

▪ ▪ ▪

One major difference exists between offline and online when it comes to attracting the attention of mothers. The use of the Internet as a marketing tool affords you the opportunity to rapidly change your strategy. It allows you to communicate in an almost instantaneous way with your customers. Whether you decide to become a content provider or e-tailer targeting mothers, use the Internet to conduct a meaningful conversation with your consumer. Remember, once they start talking to you, they will talk about you to others. There is a great deal to be gained by capturing a mother's attention online. The good news is that moms are only a few keystrokes away from connecting with you and your product. The only thing left to do now is help them find you out there in the vast frontier of the worldwide Web.

## CHAPTER SIX

# Generating Mom's Clicks Online

T HE LAST CHAPTER focused on developing an effective Web site. In this chapter, we'll explore how to get customers to your Web page. The Internet presents a remarkable opportunity to connect with millions of mothers. You can speak to your customers 24 hours a day, seven days a week in one-on-one interactions that exist in a real-time environment. You have the opportunity to evaluate a mom's response to your latest marketing efforts almost immediately. In the past, a toy company might send out a postcard announcing a sale on a particular new product and wait several days to see if sales increase. Today, the same toy store owner can put up a "sale" banner on his site and within hours determine if his value proposition is enough to get people to buy.

Although the Internet is a wonderful communication vehicle, helping customers find you can be difficult. It is estimated that in 2000 there were over 550 billion pages on the Web.[1] So how do mothers find your Web site? This is where a strong online marketing strategy becomes important.

Michael Egan, founder of Alamo Rent A Car and chairman of theglobe.com, believes that *distribution* is the single most important thing to obtain on the Internet. I believe he is correct. The way to build a brand online is to be in as many places as much as possible. Fortunately, many tactical strategies cost you more in time than money and will help you meet this goal.

# Achieving Distribution

SEARCH ENGINES, CONTENT syndication, e-newsletters, banner exchanges and purchases, link swapping, pay for click programs, affiliate programs, and online community involvement are just a few of the marketing initiatives that will create distribution for your company.

Again, I would caution that you pay as much attention to targeting the right market online as you would offline. For example, you wouldn't place a full-page ad for breast pumps in *Field and Stream* magazine. Apply the same philosophy online. Sometimes less is better, particularly on the Internet, where you can spend money on a small site with a targeted market and get better results than spending lots of money on sites with large fragmented markets.

For instance, EF Au Pair, one of the nation's largest au pair services, recently told me that one of their most successful marketing campaigns was one in which they targeted mothers of twins. With this in mind, EF Au Pair would be wise spending marketing dollars with sites such as TwinsAdvice.com. Although TwinsAdvice.com does not have the hundreds of thousands of moms coming to their site that Parents.com does, they do have an extremely active message board of loyal mothers of multiples. Advertising on TwinsAdvice.com would give EF

# Top Twenty Sites for Mothers*

| Web Site | Unique Visitors | Composition (%) |
|---|---|---|
| melaleuca.com | 86,000 | 91 |
| pantene.com | 134,000 | 74 |
| babiesonline.com | 272,000 | 65 |
| makestuff.com | 208,000 | 65 |
| rbclick.com | 171,000 | 64 |
| thefamilycorner.com | 117,000 | 63 |
| couponmaker.com | 135,000 | 63 |
| webcertificate.com | 85,000 | 62 |
| longaberger.com | 143,000 | 60 |
| walmartphotocenter.com | 99,000 | 60 |
| fisherpricestore.com | 172,000 | 58 |
| currentcatalog.com | 107,000 | 57 |
| parents-and-kids.com | 175,000 | 56 |
| myavon.com | 227,000 | 56 |
| pamperedchef.com | 174,000 | 55 |
| ipads.com | 99,000 | 55 |
| couponparadise.com | 136,000 | 53 |
| netjewels.com | 150,000 | 53 |
| familytime.com | 215,000 | 53 |
| free-beauty-samples.com | 92,000 | 52 |

*According to composition of women age eighteen+ with children present.

Sample Size: Approximately 60,000 individuals throughout the United States.

Composition: The percentage of a web site/channel/application's visitors that belong to a specific age/gender grouping.

*Source:* Media Metrix, December 2001.

Au Pair a much greater return for its investment. It might be the same for a formula company such as Ross Laboratories. If you win the loyalty of a mother with twins, you gain twice the return with a single investment of marketing dollars.

As the chapter proceeds, we'll look at some sites that are successfully attracting mothers and learn from their experience.

BlueSuitMom.com, for example, started as many do, with a frugal marketing budget. We can now afford to spend more on online marketing but because of the successful results of our initial marketing plan, we have not increased our online marketing budget significantly. In fact, Rachael Bender and I use BlueSuitMom.com as a marketing guinea pig for some BSM Media clients. BlueSuitMom.com is a good example of how you can build a brand and significant Web traffic by wisely selecting your online marketing elements and applying a focused strategy.

# Online Newsletters

"THE MOST EFFECTIVE way we've found to get people to come back to our sites and those of our clients is through weekly newsletters," says Bender. "Within 24 hours of sending out a newsletter we typically see a 30 to 40 percent spike in traffic, especially to the items mentioned in the newsletter. What makes our newsletters so successful? Every issue delivers useful information about topics important to the audience whether it is working mothers, new moms, or moms of teenagers; we never include information that isn't pertinent to our readers. I would rather send out a newsletter with two items than waste the valuable time of our readers. What will

# BSM Media's Recommended Low-Cost Online Marketing Tools

■ Trade a link to your site with other retail Web sites.

■ Exchange banners, newsletter ads, button ads with other Web site operators.

■ Distribute your content with a link back to your site to other Web sites.

■ Conduct a sweepstakes on your site and get it listed on sweepstake sites.

■ Offer free samples and get these listed in freebie newsletters.

■ Mention your site in postings on message boards that relate to your subject matter.

■ Allow your audience to share your site with others by posting a "refer this page to a friend" tool on every page.

■ Submit your site to Web site reviewers in order to be posted as "the best" in your category.

set you apart is delivering valuable advice along with your sales information.

"For instance, when producing the electronic newsletter for a baby products online store, we might explain the basics of how to know when an infant is sick and then recommend a good thermometer. Or if we were giving advice on how to lose weight after pregnancy, we'd recommend a jogging stroller. Even if the person isn't interested in buying the thermometer yet, they still read our newsletter for the valuable information it contains. The next time that subscriber is looking for a childcare product our client will be the first company they think of. Another bonus of newsletters is that these people have already been to your Web site and were interested in your product. They are a pre-qualified group for your advertising message," explains Bender.

# Advertising in Other Newsletters

WE'VE ALSO BEEN successful at attracting new working mothers to BlueSuitMom.com by advertising in other people's newsletters. We can purchase advertising ranging anywhere from $50 to $500 an issue depending on the number of subscribers. When looking for newsletters to advertise in, remember to focus on finding newsletters that contain your demographics. If you know most of your customers are new mothers, it will not be effective to advertise in a newsletter that has 60 percent of its audience as men. Before buying any advertising, subscribe to the newsletters for a couple weeks to determine if their tone fits in with your advertising message.

Another successful marketing initiative is to get selected pieces of content on other sites. They often have a broader audience than our niche but this allows a funnel effect to take place in identifying our target. Most Web sites are constantly looking for quality content. If you're knowledgeable in a particular field, consider writing articles or columns for other Web sites. Ask that they include a short blurb about your site or product and a link to your Web site at the end of each article. We worked with a pediatrician who produced a video on potty training so we turned her video script into an informative piece of written content on the same subject.

The article on successful potty training was offered to parenting sites and baby sites as well as female-oriented Web sites. A little creativity resulted in millions of moms viewing her article on the Discovery Channel's TLC program site.

Your content doesn't only have to be articles. Mothers like lists that limit their choices. How about a list of the top ten questions to ask when determining if your child is ready to begin using the potty or the top ten children's apparel colors for 2002?

As another example, Bob Hunter, CEO of Stork Avenue, was seeing firsthand the anxiety new mothers go through when trying to select the perfect name for their baby, so he wrote an article on what goes into naming your baby. He used the article on his site, and BSM Media distributed it to other pregnancy and parenting sites. The article put his logo and link in front of thousands of expectant mothers outside of StorkAvenue.com.

## The Importance of Links

CONTENT IS NOT the only thing you can swap to generate traffic to your site. "Developing a network of other small businesses who are willing to add a link from their Web site to yours and vice versa is a great way to get free advertising and develop relationships with other entrepreneurs," says Bender. Swap advertising space in one another's newsletters or put a banner ad on a strategic place. For instance, if you run a mail-order gift cake company, you could team up with a florist to add links from your order confirmation page to the florist. They would then add a link from their confirmation page. Find companies to exchange links with by finding out where your competitor is getting links. Just type in link:URL (for example, link:bluesuitmom.com) in a search engine and you can find all the pages linking to that Web site.

Links to your site are also important because some search engines determine placement based on a formula that includes the number of links going to and from your site. Search engines are one of the most valuable sources of web traffic but getting your site listed near the top can be tricky. Successful Web sites almost always credit their traffic to where they appear in Yahoo!, Google, AltaVista, and others. There are several good online resources for information about search-engine positioning (www .searchenginewatch.com, for example) and articles about search engines at ClickZ (http://clickz.com/column/seo.html).

Don't think you are going to submit your site to the various search engines once and be done with it. I have seen this mistake made too many times. I worked with a travel company a few years ago that had two dozen people working daily on updating their site, creating promotions to sell trips, and changing elements to make their site more flashy, but they had no, and I mean no, search-engine strategy. Day after day, they sat in strategy meetings to figure out why sales were down and they had no traffic while their site didn't even appear in the first five pages of a search for vacations. Search-engine placement as a marketing tool means weekly if not daily execution. But the fruits of your labor can be great. Earning top placement in a category that meets your market can drive hundreds of thousands of mothers to your site.

# Pay-for-Placement Sites

THE IMPORTANCE OF good search-engine placement is evident in the popularity of pay-for-placement sites such as Overture.com. This company allows advertisers to bid for placement in its search results on terms that they select. The search results are then distributed to tens of thousands of sites across the Internet, including Yahoo!, America Online, Terra Lycos, and AltaVista. Advertisers pay Overture the amount of their bid only when a consumer clicks on their listing, providing a cost-effective way to drive targeted customer leads to their sites. Overture allows you to select the search terms that are most important to your business and control your spending through the bidding process. For instance, you may be willing to pay .50 per lead for each mother searching for baseball gloves but you only have a $2,000 budget. Your Overture account will continue to place you in the search results for "baseball gloves" at .50 per click until you use up your $2,000 budget. After your account is depleted, you either deposit more into the account or let your placement expire.

The bidding process, however, can get heated and may stack you up against big spenders. For instance, in the category of Women's Health, bids can be as high as $1.40+ per lead. At that rate, $2,000 will not go very far. Select your bid categories wisely and monitor the bidding screens to learn whom you are bidding against. Many smaller companies find success by bidding on less popular yet relevant terms. Karen Wilkinson, president of eBubbles.com, bids on product names that are unique to her product line, such as Eucalyptus soaps. This strategy gives her a better chance to win high placement in some soap categories.

## AVOID TRICKY MARKETING

There are a few things to consider when using Overture. First, be considerate of your customer's patience. Many bidders drive traffic to their home page rather than the page on their site that features the desired product in the search term. As an example, a child's apparel retailer wins high placement in the search term "toddler shorts," but when a potential customer clicks on their search term, the link takes the customer to a home page of all toddler clothing, forcing the potential customer to navigate through products they are not interested in. This tactic erodes the trust of your potential customers. If you want Overture traffic to gain exposure to your entire product line, then evaluate the layout of your site to present other merchandise in an organized manner on all product pages. This can easily be done through left or right rail navigation or a top navigation bar containing product categories. This way your mother goes directly to "toddler shorts" but see that you also sell "toddler shirts." Overture is extending a watchful eye toward marketers conducting this unfriendly and tricky marketing, so if you don't change it yourself, they will probably tell you to change it soon.

## GET WHAT YOU PAY FOR

Be careful of the bidding process. I've seen bidding on Overture have the same effect as bidding on Ebay or playing a Vegas slot machine. Make sure the time and money you are spending are producing the results you are looking for. If it's sales, determine what the cost of a sale is for traffic coming from your pay-for-placement investment. If you are spending $400 a day on Overture or others but receiving $1,500 a day in sales, then you are doing the right thing. On the flip side, if you are only making $100 in sales, then something is not working. It could be the layout of your site or the terms you are purchasing, but the reality is that it is not producing the right results for you.

Bob Hunter at Stork Avenue uses Overture religiously and uses it well. He sets a weekly budget for pay-for-placement sites and monitors traffic and sales daily. He can literally show you in any given hour what sales are coming in from search terms, the sales per customer, and the margin on each purchase. Not everyone has Bob's sophisticated technology, but even the smallest operation can monitor traffic and sales.

Darcy Miller of BabyGiftStore.com uses search optimizing to send mothers to her site. She takes the process a step further by creating keyword intense mini-sites within BabyGiftStore.com. Miller explains that her team will create a mini-site for keepsake jewelry by grouping together the same type of products in their inventory. This strategy allows the potential customer to see all jewelry when they land on the keepsake jewelry site. The strategy also works in her favor with traditional search-engine submissions as well. When search-engine spiders comb her site, they find the related keyword several times on the page giving that page higher placement in their search engine.

Miller also has been successful in driving mothers to her other original Web site, LittleDidIKnow.com, a site filled with much of the same product as BabyGiftStore.com.

Says Miller, "I would recommend hiring someone to do search-engine management. It is a time-consuming task that has to be monitored almost daily, and it requires the tricks of the trade. Every search engine has different standards by which they catalog sites and they change them often. There are people out there whose job it is to engineer your site and the code on each page in a way that it is more attractive to the search engines."

According to Miller, it's critical to be listed within the first couple of pages of a search engine; otherwise, "you'll be buried in a sea of Web sites, and no one will take the time to find you." Without search engine traffic, you are left to rely on the links that you've scattered throughout the Web. One trick, says Miller, is to scatter your links anywhere and everywhere you can because some search engines assign higher placements to sites based on the number of links to the site. Make it a habit to list your site in at least three places a day. A great place to find literally thousands of places to list your site is at www.the1000.com. Make it very easy for visitors to link to you. Have a special place where they can easily find your buttons and banners because those will stand out and be an actual ad. "We also have an opt-in e-mail list so that we can send our visitors updates, specials, and newsletters to increase repeat traffic and buying," explains Miller.

"Recently we have also begun monitoring expired URLs on URLBargains.com. Sometimes these URLs have good positioning on search engines although they are presently a dead link. That happened to us recently with a URL, www.babyandtoddlergifts.com. I went to Yahoo! and realized that it was number one in the search engine so I bought it and redirected traffic to babygiftstore.com. There are many URLs expiring now so you can pick up good Web sites names for far less than a few years ago."

Miller has engaged mothers not only as customers but also as business partners through her banner exchanges and links. She now has a lot of moms talking about her and her companies in a number of ways.

# A Marketing Tool with a Viral Effect

SINCE MOMS LIKE to share and we want them to talk about our product or Web site, reward them for this behavior by including a "send this page to a friend" tool on your site. It's a great online marketing tool that can create a viral effect. By adding a "send this page to a friend" feature, you make it easier for moms to share your great product or Web site with others. My partner, Rachael Bender, recommends either using a free version of recommending script hosted by another Web site (like www.recommend-it.com) or creating your own cgi script. We suggest that you add the "send this page to a friend" feature to every page on your site. Such high traffic sites as Bellaonline.com and Parents.com use this successful method.

# Case Studies: Examining Successful Strategies

MANY WEB SITE marketers apply these methods along with their own creativity to successfully generate traffic to their site. Several of the success stories, like hbwm.com and Amazingmoms.com, started out as single-person operations with small marketing budgets that have grown into well-known online brands. They are proof that a well-conceived online marketing plan can work in generating traffic to your site. Let's take a look at what has built their success.

## HOME-BASED WORKING MOTHERS

Lesley Spencer, founder of Home-Based Working Mothers, a Web site designed for mothers who run home-based businesses (www.hbwm.com), has been able to gain the attention of mothers as customers and business partners. Her site provides information and resources to the 5 million mothers who are running businesses from their homes. She relates to mothers as customers and marketing partners by using many of them as contributing writers. There's nothing like a proud female with an article on a well-respected Web site to deliver additional traffic (she'll tell all her friends). Spencer also utilizes other marketing initiatives to reach her market.

"Our most successful online marketing initiative has been search engine listings. The highest amount of our traffic from any one source has been Yahoo!, which has sent us about 13 percent of our traffic. The next highest (11 percent) is from folks typing in our domain from word-of-mouth referrals, publicity, and bookmarks. I would say that overall 40 to 50 percent of our traffic is from search engines. We manually listed ourselves with the main search engines and used a service to submit our URL to several of the smaller ones." Spencer also offers a biweekly e-newsletter that includes articles, tips, and information regarding parenting and working from home. She makes sure that the content is relevant and fairly short. "E-newsletters are offered freely all over the Internet," says Spencer, "so you need to give them a reason to subscribe as well as a reason to stay subscribed." To encourage sign-ups, Spencer has a registration box on her home page and includes subscribing information in the e-newsletter itself and in the signature line of her email.

## Amazing Moms

Kit Bennett, founder of Amazingmoms.com, attracts thousands of mothers seeking solutions to the age-old challenge, "How do I keep my child busy and having fun at the same time?" Her site presents pages of fun activities, birthday party ideas, and art projects. All are ideas that mothers can share with other moms, creating a great opportunity for Amazingmoms.com. Bennett uses several marketing ideas to capitalize on her loyal mothers.

"Our e-mail newsletter has been a great marketing tool. A successful e-mail newsletter should provide the reader with something useful, not just advertising. Amazingmoms' newsletter offers crafts, parenting tips, and recipe ideas. The goal is to get readers to click through to your Web site so don't provide the entire article in your newsletter. Introduce your information with an alluring sentence or two and then add a link to 'read more.' Write for your readers. Send your newsletter regularly and in a consistent format. You want to create habit in your reader so that they become dependent upon the information you provide them. People receive hundreds of emails each day, so you don't want to overwhelm them by sending your newsletter too often. Weekly seems to work well for Amazingmoms. The Internet allows you to interact with your customers so create interaction with games or contests."

Bennett gets viewers to register for her e-newsletter with different tactics. She promotes a monthly prize drawing for new members, includes sign-up notices in the first screen on her site, and adds her newsletter ad to her e-mail signature. Says Bennett, "Make it easy for people to subscribe to your newsletter. A reader should be able to subscribe by simply typing their e-mail and getting a welcome message for a confirmation."

Although in the beginning Bennett tried to manage the Amazingmoms list in-house, she now uses a list management company that charges about $30.00/month to send

5,000 newsletters, an investment she believes is well worth it to eliminate the hassle of doing it herself.

"Look for companies that can manage all subscriptions and 'unsubscribe,' have the capability to gather demographics, allow the list owner to add several e-mails at one time, and have HTML format capabilities," says Bennett.

When looking for links, Bennett first searches for sites within her target market, but not direct competitors. "I take the time to get to know the site, find contact information, and a name if possible. I take notes about the site so that I personalize my correspondence," explains Bennett. "For example, if I'm at an education site, I might take note of a particular lesson plan I liked. After I've gathered 100 or so e-mails I write a letter expressing my appreciation for what they have created in their site and my desire to exchange links with them."

Bennett's research is time-consuming but she finds it to be well worth the effort. "I have found that all of my links have provided a lasting relationship and improve my standings on the search engines. I do not recommend mass mailings. As the Webmaster of Amazingmoms.com, I ignore most of the generic mailings but always respond to the letters with a personal touch," says Bennett.

The personal touch that Bennett adds to her marketing plan comes through in her content as well as the customer attention she gives to her audience. It is the key contributor to the loyalty she has gained with her audience.

## SURE FIT INC.

Another company who has won the loyalty of their customers through customer service is Sure Fit Inc., the country's leading furniture-cover manufacturer. Sure Fit's online marketing plan varies from the sites we have looked at thus far. Instead of marketing to mothers directly through its site with content and newsletters, it lingers in places that moms hang out on the Internet.

"Slipcovers are a wonderful solution for mothers," says Fae Guerin, Internet marketing manager for Sure Fit. "However, instead of marketing to mothers specifically, we've chosen to target sites whose demographics fit our profile. That includes anything from portals and search engines to decorating, shopping, and catalog sites. Mothers hang out at all of these places. Our best partners include Catalog City, Biz Rate, and Shop At Home," explains Guerin, who also uses Overture for pay-for-performance search engine results. "We've begun partnering with affinity sites to present e-mail offers to each other's subscribers. These partners include sites such as DecorateToday.com, Fieldcrest.com, Furniture Fan.com, MarthaStewart.com, Signals Catalog, and others."

Sure Fit is about to launch an affiliate program, which may include charity sites such as iGive and GreaterGood, a school fundraiser site like SchoolPop.com, or reward sites like MyPoints and E-Centives. Again, these are places where moms choose to shop.

## EF Au Pair

EF Au Pair, which has been providing intercultural childcare since 1989, uses offline marketing campaigns to drive traffic to their Web site. Susan Robinson, vice president of Marketing at EF Au Pair, describes their online marketing efforts. "One of the most well-received campaigns we conducted was a direct mail postcard driving recipients to our Web site. When on the site, if they refer three friends, the referring family received 'the working family survival kit,' which contained things like a coloring book, post-it notes, first aid kit, travel mug, crayons." The referral process gets mothers talking to each other about you and it becomes viral. Another successful marketing initiative is their "Recipes for Life," short uplifting hints which EF Au Pair e-mails to their client families. Says Robinson, "They seem to value the content enough to forward them to friends and family thus spreading our name."

Robinson's marketing partner, Sean McGonagle, director of Marketing for EF Au Pair, adds that they also have a presence in search engines. "We purchase keywords such as nanny, babysitters, au pair, and childcare. We also work with well-known sites such as parenthood.com, careguide.com, and carefinder.com by creating business development relationships. The connection with these sites solidifies EF Au Pair as a viable childcare alternative, especially when they link articles on the topic back to us. Online advertorial is a good strategy for us because it allows us to talk about the positives of using au pairs."

# Tools That Drive Traffic to Your Site

MANY LOW-COST TOOLS exist to drive traffic to your site, particularly when targeting mothers. The most effective target a women's natural desire to find value, try new products, share ideas, compare results, and give their opinions.

## SWEEPSTAKES

Everyone loves to win a prize and moms are no different. They particularly like items that benefit their family, such as family vacations or prizes aimed at pampering themselves, such as spa visits or bubble bath kits.

Make your drawing or contest easy to register, limit your restrictions, make sure you have all the necessary elements (including guidelines for certain states), and make sure you only ask for information that you really need. Nothing will drive a mother away from your site faster than asking for too much information. We all want demographic information from our audience but be sure you know what you intend to do with it. Too many questions make your audience bored and suspicious. Ultimately you will drive them away and they will rarely return to give you a second chance. When reviewing consumer questionnaires, I ask myself after reading each question, "Why am I asking this and what do I intend to do with the information if they give it to me?" For example, unless I intend to fax promotional materials to my database of subscribers, it is a waste of time to ask my customers their fax number.

This rule applies to online surveys as well.

## POLLS

As we have already learned, mothers like to give their opinion, and for that reason online polls on your site are a good marketing tool. Polls not only provide you with something to use in a press release but they get mothers talking to and about you. Moms will forward poll pages in an effort to let other moms also voice their opinions. The trick is to ask relevant and engaging questions. For instance, on BlueSuitMom .com, we ask questions regarding work and family balance, such as: "What work/life benefit would you like most?"

"Who cares for your children while you are at work?" "Is your employer family-friendly?" "Which flexible work option appeals to you?"

We use the results from these polls to attract the attention of the press as well. Each year BlueSuitMom.com releases a list of the most desired Mother's Day gifts, which is generated from our online survey of mothers. We are in good company when it comes to using online polls. You can also find online polls on sites such as Clubmom.com, RBClick .com, and iVillage.com. Surveys are a fun, interactive element of a Web site and incorporating instant-results capability keeps your audience engaged. Particularly with the mom market, these tools work well. Remember the park scene at the beginning of this book? Moms love to compare and share. Online surveys allow mothers to see what other moms think, instantaneously.

Surveys are a great way to gather demographic information about your audience. "How many times a week do you cook dinner?" can tell you if they are spending a lot of time in the kitchen, if they have a need for recipes and cooking information, if they are spending a great deal of money eating out, and if they frequent restaurants. If you are a consumer-product company with food brands and a survey shows that your audience is only cooking two nights a week, you might add quick and easy recipes using your product to your site. The convenience you incorporate into using your product will not only generate incremental sales but also create customer loyalty. Where do you think a mom is going to go next time she wishes she had time to cook a nice dinner for her family? Back to your quick recipes, of course.

■ ■ ■

The Internet brings together many essential elements for marketers and advertisers who want to reach mothers. It puts us in a pool filled with mothers ready and willing to talk with us. All we have to do is present them with a well-designed Web site with relevant solutions and engage them in a conversation, an activity they enjoy. As we have learned in this chapter, the Internet gives us hundreds of ways to get the conversations started. It's now up to you to decide where to extend your efforts in order to create your most successful dialogues with mothers.

## CHAPTER SEVEN

# Marketing to Moms Through the Mail

Each evening when I arrive home from work, four small, eager faces greet me, each struggling to be the first to tell me about their day. Each child applies their own strategy to reach their goal. The strategy of my three-year-old daughter, Morgan, seems to work the best. She merely whines until I pick her up to gain a reprieve from the constant half cry, half moan tone that she produces. Keenan, six years old, retreats to the bedroom where he jumps on my bed in anticipation that I will soon be there, changing out of my work clothes. Some of our most meaningful conversations have occurred with me in various states of undress with his body bobbing between the ceiling and the mattress. Owen, who is eight, will just yell from the couch while watching sports with his dad or between Nintendo games. Madison, my other eight year old, will continue to play quietly with her animals on the dining room table, seemingly not attune to all the chaos. What I've learned about Madison is that she is just silently taking it all in and will replay it to me at a moment when it's calm and I'm approachable.

Also waiting to greet me is a pile of mail stacked haphazardly on a table near the stairs. Magazines, bills, credit card offers, and direct mail pieces are all randomly meshed together, waiting for me to respond.

In reality there is not much difference between the strategies that my children employ to gain my attention and those pieces of mail that sit on my table. Their goals are certainly the same. Both want to gain my attention. Whether it is a catalog, product introduction, or magazine, each piece of mail is intended to drive a behavior in me as a consumer, mother, businesswoman, or wife. Just as each of my children execute a different tactic to get their message across, so do the creators of these printed materials.

Some might inundate me with constant noise like my three year old, although theirs comes in the way of special offers and weekly direct mail pieces. This method is used commonly by credit card companies, whose direct marketing strategy is a numbers game based on a constant stream of mailbox noise. More creative marketers share Keenan's strategy. They position themselves in a place and time that assures them of my attention. Seasonal catalogs are a good example. Wooden Soldier, a children's clothing retailer, does a good job of using this tactic. In March, when it is time for me to shop for the children's Easter clothes, I'll receive one of their catalogs. Rather than send me catalogs twelve times a year, which would be extremely expensive, they wait until they know my attention is on buying their product. Toys "R" Us also does this with seasonal brochures of toys, although I would tend to say that they use a combination of high frequency and seasonal relevance. Magazines tend to take the approach of Madison, my silent but knowledgeable child.

They arrive in your mailbox on a regular schedule and will perhaps sit in the pile for a while, waiting for you to take the time to flip through the pages. Just as I learn a great deal from Madison once we find a quiet moment to connect, I know that there will be meaningful connections with the content and advertisers in the magazines. The last and least successful strategy (when applied to direct mail at least) is Owen's tactic of screaming at me every once in a while with different messages. These direct mail pieces are unexpected, show little relevance to my life, and may even represent a product or service I've never heard of. It works for Owen because he already owns my heart, but it doesn't work for advertisers. In fact, this tactic often leaves the recipient wondering why she received it at all. These are the pieces that go immediately into the garbage can.

I like to think that my household is not that far from the reality of most households with children in America. I think the fact that many moms refer to the hours between 5 P.M. and 7 P.M. as the bewitching hours helps me to feel confident that the Bailey household is not much different than the Wanezek's home in Wisconsin, the Gold's home in Maryland, or the Madsen's in Idaho. Moms don't have a lot of spare time to go through mail that doesn't immediately capture their attention. Just as my own children have learned, it's important to initiate a strategy that is going to get the best results for you when it comes to mom's attention.

# Catalogs

CATALOGS DESIGNED TO meet the needs of mothers are one strategy that can mean sales. Revenue generated from catalog sales to mothers is big business. According to the National Mail Order Association (www.nmoa.org), mail-order related sales in the United States exceeded $1.7 trillion in 2000. The amount spent on toys, games, and children's products through mail order was over $2 billion during the same year. In fact, 69 percent of consumers buy from catalogs and moms are a large part of that market. Almost 13 percent of mail-order apparel sales are in the category of children's clothing and over 3.3 million people purchased baby accessories via mail order. Female catalog consumers ages twenty-six to thirty-five spent the most on children's items, while mothers ages thirty-six to forty-five came in a close second.[1] All of this adds up to sales for marketers who successfully win the hearts of the mom market.

## VISUALS

Let's examine those elements that appeal to mothers. Catalogs targeting mothers should, like print advertising, contain designs that allow a mother to picture herself or a member of her family in the product. A lot of children's retailers use large pictures of smiling children. Mothers love to see their children smiling. Children's Wear Digest, CWD, differentiated itself from other spring 2002 catalogs by using a collage of smiling children. The technique not only set their cover apart but also allowed them to quickly show moms the variety of sizes, shapes, and styles the catalog contained. It was a good strategy for speaking to the time restraints of a busy mother. It lets the mother determine that the catalog is relevant whether she has a toddler or a preteen because all are pictured on the cover.

## A Call to Action

Another ingredient necessary for catalogs geared toward mothers is the call to action. The best catalogs make it easy by offering a variety of ways to buy. These can include fax, online e-commerce, telephone orders, and mail. A mother doesn't have the time to find your phone number in fine print. Include your phone number and Web-site address on each and every page of your catalog in a consistent location so when a mother dog-ears a page with desired merchandise, she has everything she needs on that page to order your product.

## The Issue of Trust

Mothers want to know that they are spending their household money wisely and that you will stand behind your product and service. They also want to know that they can trust you to help them buy efficiently. In a catalog, or any direct mail piece, you can establish trust by clearly displaying return policies, forms of payment, shipping information, gift-wrapping details, and customer guarantees. The more information you provide to your customer, the less she will suspect you are hiding. Disclose your privacy policy. Even if you don't intend to sell your customer list, tell your readers that. It will go a long way to making them feel like they are doing business in a safe environment.

# Case Studies: Appealing Catalogs

EACH DAY HUNDREDS of catalogs line mailboxes across the United States. Although many will never make it farther than the foyer wastebasket, the successful ones will generate millions of dollars in sales. As we have done with other marketing tools, let's take a look at catalogs that are working to gain the attention of the mom market.

## eBubbles

eBubbles.com is an online retailer that specializes in bath, body care, and wellness products from around the world. The irregular small size and clean white cover of eBubbles' catalog quickly caught my attention. Rather than using a large busy image, the cover features a great deal of white space with a single bar of soap. The pages were laid out in an easy-to-browse format with product organized by country of origin.

Karen Wilkinson, founder and president of eBubbles.com, says the irregular use of size and graphics was intentional. "We used a lot of white space to give readers a free feeling that created the sense of relaxing reading. Those free and relaxing feelings are the same feelings that our customers experience after using our product. The rule of thumb for covers is don't try to pitch product on the cover in order to avoid tying your brand to just one product, thus limiting consumer appeal. It might seem that we broke the rule by featuring a single bar of soap on the cover, but soap is part of our branding. So we used the soap and white space to brand our company. We used colors to reinforce the mood of the book." eBubbles selected a soothing blue-toned ink, making sure there was enough black in it to make it easy to read. According to Wilkinson, it's rude to present copy that readers can't read. "Our sales approach is calm and not pushy," says

Wilkinson. "We decided on the smaller $6^{1}/_{2}$ by $6^{1}/_{2}$ size to set the catalog apart from others, but it did require additional postage because of the square shape. Make sure to consider size and postage requirements when designing your piece."

"The back cover is prime real estate so it should contain an offer that speaks to a mother's desire to find value," continues Wilkinson. "We purposely positioned fun, colorful, and impulsive items near the back of the catalog to capture the attention of the masses that flip through pages back to forward. If we can get their interest while they are leisurely flipping, then they will take the time to read the catalog later front to back like a magazine. We were also careful to remember that over time catalog shoppers train themselves to ignore the first few pages of a magazine. For this reason, the more expensive products are put at the front of the catalog and the impulse items go in the back just as they are placed near the check-out lane in a store. Organizing your product well is a very important part of driving sales." Customers liked what they saw in eBubble's winter 2001 catalog. Wilkinson and her team printed 10,000 copies and mailed them to registered customers and others in their database instead of using a blind list. Their reported sales outpaced the direct mail average 1 percent response rate by exceeding a 3 to 5 percent return, excellent for direct mail. Pricing and product information are among the elements she attributes to eBubbles' success.

"We made certain to keep our product offering within a price point that our market could afford," says Wilkinson. "Mothers are price conscious. To help set the perceived value of our product, we included information about the country of origin and ingredients. Our popular anchor brands served as the foundation of our offering and around those products we added exotic and unusual items."

In eBubbles' next catalog, Wilkinson intends to take a lesson from Victoria's Secret, which she thinks is the queen of catalogs. "On each and every catalog they include some type of special offer on the front cover. Their 'dollar off' type of promotion works much better than a free gift offer because it gives the customer the opportunity to choose their reward. A free gift may hold no perceived value for the customer if it is something they don't want. Tiered savings is a great way to increase profitability while increasing your order size. The deal gets sweeter as the offer goes up for both you as the retailer and the customer as well," says Wilkinson.

## STORK AVENUE

Bob and Sue Hunter's Stork Avenue catalog features hundreds of original and licensed designs in a well-organized layout that invites expectant mothers to browse through pages. The feel of the catalog mirrors the excitement that an expectant mother experiences with the anticipated birth of her new baby.

In addition to establishing trust by including customer service phone numbers, e-mails, and return policies like Karen Wilkinson features in her catalog, Bob and Sue include a large color picture of the entire team at Stork Avenue. The picture not only puts a face to the company but also gives a family-feel to the catalog. In addition, a short letter from Bob and Sue adds a nice touch. The Stork Avenue catalog is also a smaller size that can easily be put in a purse or on crowded tables in hospitals or obstetrician's offices.

Each year Stork Avenue prints over 3 million catalogs that reach expectant moms through the mail, hospital bags, and prenatal classes.

## SURE FIT

Leafing through Sure Fit's catalog gives a woman the feeling that they are dealing with a girlfriend. The brightly colored pictures of Sure Fit's slipcovers in varied motifs give moms new ideas on decorating and updating the look of their old couch.

"We try to keep it friendly and value-driven," says Liana Toscanini, vice president of Insurgence at Sure Fit. "Our product lacks awareness, image, and education so we have to address all of those issues. We try to keep it simple." Toscanini educates the consumer by including a full-page, step-by-step instruction sheet for using slipcovers. The page works well because it shows a woman completing the task alone. This first lets the customer know it's an easy one-person job and second that the process is easily adaptable to any couch. The use of pictures is important to the success of this catalog.

Perhaps the best-positioned photo is a large picture on the back cover that shows a child sitting on the arm of a couch reading a book. The couch is wrapped in a Sure Fit cover and crayons and coloring books litter the floor in front of it. It's a picture that mothers can relate to and shows the practicality of the product, which speaks to value, convenience, and efficiency. Placement on the back cover ensures that it gets maximum exposure. Imagine the catalog lying cover down in a family room. A mother looks down at this beautiful picture and then looks up at her own boring old family room. Immediately she has visions of transforming it into a catalog picture.

Another original feature on Sure Fit's back cover is a small picture of a woman shopping online on SureFit.com. Underneath, copy explains how you can view additional patterns and shop online. It is a creative way to promote their Web site and encourage mothers to visit.

Before we leave the Sure Fit brand, I'd like to mention another piece of Sure Fit's printed marketing material—the Sure Fit slipcover Instructions and Guide. Similar to their catalog, the booklet features pretty pastel pages with an unusually cut index-type cover. Each tab corresponds to a particular part of the book, such as ruffled skirt instructions, slipcover sizing, ongoing care, and decorating with slipcovers. To make it easy for mothers, the instruction pages contain numbered step-by-step, how-to pictures. It is an informative piece designed in an easy-to-read style that speaks to every concern a mother would have in using a slipcover.

## LittleDidIKnow

The most unique catalog I've ever seen was produced by Darcy Miller and the moms of LittleDidIKnow.com in 1999 and is an example of how creativity doesn't always work to generate sales. LittleDidIKnow.com features the products and services of over forty mothers. The products range from keepsake jewelry to wall mural kits. Miller realized that each of her mothers had an interesting story that brought them to developing their product. The catalog included a short profile on each mother and a description of her product. Each story left the reader with a "wow" feeling. Each mom's profile also featured a picture of the mother with her children. You couldn't help but read the stories behind each product.

"The idea was to give mom the opportunity to say here's someone just like me, they are doing it, and look at the cool products they make and sell. We gave them information as well as success stories of mothers in an attempt to connect. The catalogs were distributed in OB offices, trade shows, parks, day cares, and doctor offices and used in press kits. The catalog became one big mom's networking group," says Miller.

The catalogs caught the attention of both Oprah and Rosie, who featured some of the LittleDidIKnow.com mothers on their shows. They also opened a lot of doors for public awareness and appreciation for moms and their ideas. What they didn't do was generate a lot of sales. Miller admits that although the message of "created by moms" is a unique angle, it doesn't always send the right message.

"Moms don't have confidence yet in mom-owned businesses," says Miller. "They think because it is owned by a mom that the company owner is in her garage somewhere putting Popsicle sticks together with glue." Miller features the same products on her secondary Web site, BabyGiftStore.com, with no mention of the fact that they are produced by moms, and sales are consistently higher than on LittleDidIKnow.com. "I know some of that can be attributed to the URL but a lot has to do with consumer perception," explains Miller.

Although the catalog was creative and featured moms, it didn't take into consideration the *needs* of moms. When it comes to products for their family, moms want reliability and to know that a company stands behind the products. They didn't find that in the mom-made products of the LDIK catalog.

# Case Studies:
# Successful Direct Mail Approaches

DIRECT MAIL PIECES range from simple postcards to elaborately enveloped packets of information. Professionals dedicated to the art of effective direct sales will advise you on such tricks as clean white envelopes that carry no company identification to FedEx-looking packages. These widely used effects are easily identified and scream out irrelevant junk mail. I suggest designing direct mail pieces that address a specific concern and offer mothers a solution. The solution may come in the form of special discounts, information on a new time-saving product, or easy ways to buy a product. Instead of using the outside envelope to shout about some grand prize award or fake release authorization, use the space to say something meaningful and directed to mothers. If you are sending requested information, use the white space to note, "Requested information enclosed." This message establishes your company as there to service the requests of the customer. The package says, "I'm here because you asked me to be."

Let's look at a few direct mail pieces that work well in marketing their business to moms.

## EF AU PAIR

EF Au Pair uses a direct mail packet to send parents information about their service. The packets are mailed in response to inquiries that come from a variety of sources, including their Web site. The oversized enveloped packet does a good job at establishing the company's professional image, which is particularly important for a company asking parents to trust them enough to take care of their children. The professional presentation also appeals to the taste of their more affluent clientele.

A cover letter describes the benefits of choosing an au pair as childcare, emphasizing the cultural benefits. It also addresses the screening process, which speaks to the safety concerns of selecting a day care provider. The letter also highlights the flexibility that is gained by parents when using an au pair, which is an appealing benefit for moms. Whether it is in meal planning or in scheduling, moms crave and desire flexibility.

Sharon Robinson, vice president of EF Au Pair, describes what goes into her company's printed materials. "The images we use are always smiling au pairs with a smiling child. The pictures are warm and friendly. Our main tag line, 'when you want the world for your child,' focuses on the international benefits you provide your child by having a warm, friendly au pair in your home." The materials emphasize that EF Au Pair provides high standards of childcare and that their au pairs are carefully screened.

In some areas, such as the Midwest, it is necessary to educate the market on the concept of an au pair and they lean toward more factual advertising. All of their direct mail pieces are part of a communication plan, which includes the inquiring package and a call from a local coordinator.

## THE WOMEN'S FINANCIAL NETWORK

Muriel Siebert, the Wall Street financial firm, continuously produces direct mail pieces that speak directly to women. Their e-commerce division directed at women, The Women's

Financial Network, recently mailed a direct mail brochure that focused on their CollegeBoundFund product. The piece appropriately featured a mother and her preteen daughter on the cover. The photo immediately allows a mother to picture herself in the situation. More importantly, the cover bullets five elements that address a mother's concern: tax-free accumulation, tax-free withdrawal, flexible beneficiary choice, low minimum investment, and all U.S. citizens eligible. The copy allows mothers to see that this product is attainable and that it offers a solution to helping her provide a better future for her child. The brochure positions the company as a financial partner with mothers. Considering that single mothers are the fastest growing demographic, offering a financial partner in a situation where there is likely no partner at all is a valuable solution.

## Omaha Steaks

Some of the best direct marketing initiatives, although not exclusively designed for mothers, come from Omaha Steaks. Although the steak company makes it easy for moms to do meal planning by offering recipes and product that is conveniently delivered to their door, the best execution comes from their use of personalization. Each direct sales packet is personalized and often suggests product that the customer has bought in the past. It makes selecting product easy, an example of how Omaha Steaks does some of the work for me.

The best feature occurs during November, when Omaha Steaks not only sends a holiday catalog, but also includes an order form with the contact information and order history for anyone the customer sent steaks to the prior year. For a busy mom during the holiday season, this is a welcome solution for holiday shopping. Just as Amazon.com makes it easy to order from their Web site, Omaha Steaks has created a simple ordering process for busy moms.

## MAIDS INTERNATIONAL

Results from direct mail pieces can be intensified if used in conjunction with other marketing components.

Maids International, a leader in providing team housecleaning services, executes direct marketing to businesses as well as upper-income households. Generally their market is well educated. The company executes their marketing strategy in a zone system. A zone represents a natural neighborhood. According to Corrine Beller, vice president of Marketing, their direct marketing program works like a neighborhood blitz.

"We will target an area that fits our upscale market," says Beller. "We market in a certain zone where the economy of scale is good. We saturate the neighborhood. Usually it will be a neighborhood with working professionals. Once we identify our neighborhood, we will run newspaper ads on Mondays or Tuesdays rather than Sunday when the paper is too cluttered or on Thursday when we have to compete with the food section. We also buy cable TV on networks that allow us to target our exact demographics, such as Home and Garden, Lifetime, and the Discovery Channel."

Maids International uses a tri-fold postcard for direct mail purposes. Having determined that people no longer find testimonials believable, their pieces normally contain a family with a dog with four maids cleaning in the home. According to Beller, the message that speaks to her market is "We come in, we do this right, and we deep clean your house so you don't have to."

The company also uses door hangers to reinforce their presence in the neighborhood. Door hangers are cheap to print. Says Beller, "Our teams arrive at your home in a bright yellow car, and each team member wears a uniform comprised of khakis and yellow shirts. We have come to be known as the 'yellow car company.' It is a very good billboard for us because potential customers see the yellow car sitting in the driveway of a friend's home for several hours and then they find a door hanger on their door with information about our service. Every time a team goes to a client's home they distribute door hangers to the houses on either side of the client and the three houses across the street. Within two minutes we have done five homes."

# Magazines

MAGAZINES FIND THEIR way to the mailboxes of mothers every day and are part of the mailbox conversation companies have with the mom market. Magazines are a unique type of direct mail because rather than sell a mother one company's particular goods, they are a vehicle to present various products within a combination of content and advertising. The industry is in a state of flux. As advertising dollars shrink, publishers are closing down operations with greater frequency. Well-known titles such as *Mode* and *Working Woman* magazine are just a couple of examples of those who have recently experienced this fate. Niche market publications, such as *Working Mother, Country Living,* and *Fit Preg-*

*nancy,* are finding growth by fine-tuning their focus to meet the needs of their respective markets. While old titles are dying, some new titles are emerging and doing well. *Real Simple* magazine is just one example. With paid circulation of over 700,000 and growth that is faster than projected, *Real Simple* offers Martha Stewart-like ideas with a new-age feel, appealing to the need to simplify the complex lives we all live. *Real Simple* is particularly attractive to the professional mother who has the income to make purchases from advertisers such as Ralph Lauren and Calvin Klein. Time Inc., who publishes the magazine, was smart about launching a book that played off the need to make life simple.

They are not alone at tapping into the simple theme. *Redbook* took it one step further and added the word "balance" to their publication tag line. Above their title are now the words, BALANCING FAMILY • WORK • LOVE • TIME FOR YOU. It is a unique way to shift the focus of the title without redesigning a well-known brand.

Carol Evans, CEO of Working Mother Media, which publishes *Working Mother* magazine, sees magazines as an effective means for marketers to reach mothers. "Working mothers are in the lowest quintiles of television viewing and the highest quintiles of magazine reading of all women. Why? They are seeking information, help, and support—and they need that more than they need to be entertained. And yet marketers who need to reach mothers continue to think of television first, with magazines often an afterthought. I believe any marketer could change the relationship with working mothers overnight by shifting some or all of their television dollars to support intelligent, fun, emotionally connecting advertising in the good, old-fashioned print medium."

Finally, I cannot end without focusing on the prenatal and infant category of magazines. Although *American Baby* magazine, published by Primedia, is the oldest baby publication in the United States, newcomers seem to be entering the market every day and this saturated market continues to grow. Popular titles such as *Parents, Child,* and *Pregnancy* are jostling for space on the check-out rack with new books, including *Baby Talk, Baby Years,* and *iParenting.* The battle over capturing the attention of a busy new mother has always been fierce and I expect it to get hotter. These new publications must carve out a niche to distinguish themselves from the crowd. *Fit Pregnancy* did a good job of this in the 1990s when they launched into the prenatal market. They identified a mother's desire to stay in shape and deliver a healthy baby and focused solely on that topic. It worked because they spoke directly to the market they desired in a language the market clearly understood.

■ ■ ■

Getting your message heard above all the chatter a mother finds in her mailbox is challenging but not impossible. By designing attractive marketing pieces that distinguish your brand, speaking to your mother with relevance, and arriving at a time that creates a solution for her, your direct mail efforts can be successful. Apply the secrets of successful marketers and you will be on your way to getting your piece of the billions of dollars of mail-order sales to moms.

## CHAPTER EIGHT

# Using Special Events
# to Speak to Moms

T HERE WAS A time when my husband and I spent our
weekends combing the events calendar of our local
newspaper, looking for things to do with our children. The
goal of every Saturday and Sunday was to exhaust the energy of our toddlers and preschoolers in order to assure an
afternoon nap and a good night's sleep. Then came the day
when we enrolled them in city-sponsored team sports and
extracurricular activities and the quest for weekend activities
ended. In fact, the time we have to attend local festivals, park
events, or other non-child-initiated functions is rare. The
Bailey household is not unique in this regard; in our city, we
join hundreds of families at the ballpark each weekend. Relaxing weekends are rare for busy moms.

Consider your competition when planning special events,
particularly on the weekend, which, in the case of a family's
schedule, are not only other events but also the mother's time.
Also consider the value proposition for her or her family's attendance. Moms are special people and it's up to you to add
the "special" to your event. The good news is that your efforts

won't go unrewarded. The right event will allow you to touch a large group of your market at once with your message or branding.

Special event sponsorship can be used in a number of ways. Companies use special events to distribute samples, collect consumer data, sell product, and increase brand awareness. Special events are a good way to connect with mothers, especially events that touch their heartstrings.

# Basic Rules for Event Planning

REGARDLESS OF THE type of function you plan, a few rules apply to all special event planning. First, consider your audience's needs and interests. A free baseball clinic for mothers and their daughters probably isn't the best choice for that market. Second, consult city calendars, nonprofit event schedules, and school-vacation calendars before planning your event. I once saw a family hamburger cookout planned on a Friday during Lent. This was an event planned through the Catholic Church. Needless to say, it wasn't well attended.

Third, consider the cost of admission, particularly when targeting families. You don't want to prohibit your audience from attending. A Renaissance Festival takes place that my kids absolutely love. Unfortunately, the costs of admission and attractions are so high that it is almost as expensive as a Disney theme park. It doesn't offer the best value proposition for my family or me.

Finally, find or create an event that makes sense for your type of business or product. Luna Bars' sponsorship of fitness events makes sense to the consumer. National Car Rental sponsoring Disney events makes sense to families who rent vehicles to vacation in Orlando. *American Baby* magazine sponsoring baby fairs is easy to understand. Associating your brand with an event that has relevance and speaks to your market will go a long way in connecting with mothers.

Marilyn O'Brien of Marketing Moms adds some other thoughts to my list of rules for event sponsorship. "Look closely at categories. Event sponsorship works best with targeted audiences that allow you to understand their hot buttons. You also want to catch a mom's attention when she is at a change point. This gives you the ability to get a trail time, which is important to winning business. Baby fairs do this with new mothers. The mother is open to a change that is happening in her life. It is your opportunity to present a product that is relevant to her buying decisions," says O'Brien.

Three types of events successfully capture a mother's attention: educational events, child-oriented events, and cause-related events.

## Educational Events

EDUCATIONAL EVENTS, SUCH as seminars and conferences, give a mother the opportunity to better herself in some way to the benefit of her family. The benefit for you as a sponsor is that it positions your company as a reliable source of information in much the same way as a company who creates an information site on the Internet. If a mother gets used to relating your brand to valuable information, when she is looking for a solution to diaper rash, teething, or meal planning, she will recall your association with her learning experience.

An educational event can be conducted in any part of the country in any size market. It can be as simple as weekly parenting classes at a local elementary school or as complex as huge conferences in a convention center. Educational events can also be used to educate participants on your product. For instance, if Hershey's chocolate sponsored cooking classes, it would not be out of line for the class leader to work in desserts using Hershey's chocolate. Other educational events include lecture series, book readings, or babysitting clinics for the children of mothers. All successfully touch the heart of a mother to better herself for the sake of her family.

## SPEAKER'S BUREAUS

A strong speaker's bureau can be one of the best grassroots event-marketing initiatives a company can launch. A speaker's bureau gives you the opportunity to educate your consumers and create an awareness of your product without spending the big dollars associated with executing a large-scale event. The expense is essentially only the time of the employee scheduled to speak, although in many cases this requires after-hours or even weekend time. Organizations, clubs, and groups are always looking for speakers for their membership and networking meetings. Once word gets out that your company has an established speaker's bureau, you will have no problem keeping your speakers booked. Your biggest challenge will be accepting the engagements that best fit your marketing goals.

*Yoga Journal* is doing a good job at doing just that. The magazine's marketing efforts include event sponsorships and speaking engagements at women's conferences. The magazine conducts yoga sessions as a tool for balance and healthful living. Positioning itself as expert in the area of healthful living is a good fit for the team at *Yoga Journal* because it gives the magazine another channel of communication with its market.

## CASE STUDY: PARENTING 101

Over ten years ago, I created an event for parents called the South Florida Parenting Conference. It has since been renamed Parenting 101 and my former business partner, Meryl Guerrero, still executes the conference each year. The event was created out of the desire of my former employer, the *Miami Herald,* to gain exposure in the family market in South Florida. At the time, I was community relations manager and had access to hundreds of parenting resources. What I realized at that time and still believe today is that parents do not know where to go in their community for answers to parenting, discipline, and stress-management questions. In my capacity at the *Herald,* I knew where find these answers, so my idea was to bring parents and resources together while creating an event for the *Herald* to use to increase market share.

The one-day conference offered parents the opportunity to attend workshops and listen to speakers on topics ranging from reading to toddlers to dealing with teen issues. The event continues to draw hundreds of parents, who give up an entire Saturday to improve their parenting skills. It was an event that made sense for a newspaper to sponsor because the marketing position of a newspaper is to provide information. When budget restrictions made it impossible for the *Herald* to continue to sponsor the event, it was quickly picked up by another newspaper, confirming to us that the event was successful in reaching its goals.

## ORGANIZING AN EFFECTIVE SEMINAR

Gwen Moran of Moran Marketing Associates agrees that educational events can be an effective way to reach customers. "I think one of the most creative marketing initiatives can be found in creating a seminar that targets your market. Seminars are a powerful way to build awareness about your company, market your products or services, and possibly create a new revenue stream for your business. Seminars geared to the Mom Market can be educational venues to introduce new techniques using your product, provide mothers with a common bond with a networking opportunity, or educate expectant mothers on baby care."

# Child-Oriented Events

THERE IS NOTHING a mother loves more than seeing her child smile. She is in a constant quest to create happiness for her children and the allure of an event that can create this will earn you points. It may be a Saturday Family Fun Festival or a citywide Easter Egg Hunt. If her child has a good time, you will see sales.

I've seen a lot of great events that attract and entertain children. Chicago's Kids and Kites Festival is so popular that the mayor's office now conducts the event twice a year. The September event draws thousands of families to the steps of Chicago's Museum of Science and Industry.

Child-oriented events don't have to be large productions to gain results. One of the best events I ever attended with my children was a one-hour Lego demonstration at our local library. My children left with even more interest in Lego toys than they had originally and I felt good about spending an educational afternoon with them. When designing child-oriented events, pay attention to the time of the event and the age of the children you are targeting. It would be a major mistake to hold an event for toddlers during naptime just as it wouldn't be wise to schedule a school-age event on Saturday morning

## Creating In-Store Events

AN IN-STORE EVENT can attract mothers by giving the impression that something special is happening. Often the event is created around a sale or product introduction. These types of events appeal to the value-conscious mother. When combined with a VIP program, they truly make a mom feel special. Many retailers are capitalizing on in-store events. Neiman Marcus has In-Circle events to recognize their best customers; Macy's has pre-sale events for loyal credit card customers. Toys "R" Us is infamous for their in-store events. On a regular basis, the big-box toy retailer hosts baby fairs, toy expos, and other sales-oriented events. Create excitement for the event through newspaper circulars, store displays, magazine ads, and storefront decorations. Deep discounts and special promotional pricing entice mothers to shop now rather than later. In order to be successful, the in-store events should have a creative theme and give the perception that something very special is happening.

when many are participating in organized sports. Remember our discussion about knowing your market? This time it's beneficial to not only walk in the shoes of your target market but in the shoes of her children.

Making a splash with kids can be done without fear of drowning in expense, according to Stephanie Azzarone of Child's Play. "When targeting kids, tweens, teens—and/or their

# Great Seminars

FOLLOW THIS CHECKLIST provided by Moran Marketing Associates to make your seminars great.

- *Fee or free?* When determining what or if to charge for your seminar, consider two rules of thumb: (1) Most people attend events for which they have already paid; (2) The more you charge, the less overt your selling should be. That is, if your seminar is held primarily to showcase your expertise, you may charge higher fees. However, if you're trying to sell a specific product or service, you need to charge less or waive the fee.

- *Partner up.* Consider defraying your costs by teaming up with another related business. For example, a pediatrician and a child fitness center may deliver informative sessions on the benefits of exercise.

- *Check your date.* Do some homework to avoid competing with another event that may reduce your attendance. Call around to other facilities or city calendars to find out what they have planned for that day.

- *Determine the right length.* Before you determine the length of your seminar, consider your audience, your topic, and other related factors. If you're planning on speaking to a room full of mothers, don't schedule a full-day seminar during spring break when children are out of school. Conversely, if you have a lengthy, complex topic to discuss, don't try to cram it into a two-hour luncheon.

- *Location, location.* Most hotels and conference centers routinely host seminars and have the process down to a science. If your budget won't allow for such accommodations, check out renting space at a local college or community center.
- *Have good handouts.* Handouts are one of the most overlooked tools in seminar marketing. Give your attendees professional-looking handouts that support key points in your presentation.
- *Mini-marketing.* Create a concise marketing plan for your seminar. Include publicity, direct mail, advertising, and other appropriate promotional vehicles. Remember, the more you get the word out, the more people will attend your seminar.
- *Require an RSVP.* Advance registration gives you a good idea of how many people to expect and how many handouts you'll need. Always ask how the registrant heard about the seminar so that you can track.
- *Don't under-staff.* Be sure you have enough staff to handle registration, last-minute errands, product sales, distribution of handouts, and other essentials.
- *Capture your attendees.* Be sure that you capture names, postal and e-mail addresses, and other important contact information from your attendees for follow-up purposes. (Remember, most attendees are prospects.) You may also wish to develop a seminar evaluation form to help you make your seminar even better next time around.

# Considering Costs:
# A Checklist of Seminar Expenses

CREATING SEMINARS REQUIRES an investment of time—and money. Here is a quick budget checklist to make sure you have considered your main expenses:

- Location rental
- Food and beverage
- Lodging special guests
- Printed materials
- Event advertising
- Speaker fees
- Technical assistance and audiovisual rental
- Attendee registration packets
- Booth or expo-area fixtures
- Signage
- Shipping and postage
- Travel
- Gifts of recognition
- Take-away materials or premiums
- Personnel to staff the event

moms—special events are an ideal way to simultaneously accomplish two important goals: reach the audience directly and reach even more of them indirectly, through media."

## ORGANIZING A SUCCESSFUL CHILD-ORIENTED EVENT

For effective special events, keep the following in mind:

■ *The big idea.* What will draw consumers and press to your event? A chance to do something they couldn't otherwise, a celebrity, a good cause, free food, free admission, free products.

- *Make a list, check it twice.* Once you have a clear idea of the type of event you want, visualize every step of its implementation, from invitations to clean-up. Need to rely on outside sources for sound equipment, decorations, or other necessities? Assume nothing; confirm everything—both verbally and in writing. A small detail gone awry can be the one thing everyone will remember.

- *Location, location, location.* Select a site that will draw the public but also will be easily accessible and intriguing to media. Children's museums and toy stores are obvious choices, but don't overlook more unusual settings, from playgrounds and sports stadiums to movie theaters and concert halls. If you're targeting teens, check that your "hot spot" hasn't grown old and cold overnight.

- *Sense and sensibility.* Make sure there is a logical connection between your product and the event designed to promote it. Otherwise, neither press nor public will buy it.

- *It takes two.* Finding a co-sponsor for your event—or co-sponsoring an existing one—can dramatically cut costs. Just make sure that the public and press perceive you as the key player.

## CASE STUDY: GUND TEDDY BEARS

Azzarone's company planned and executed the centennial anniversary of Gund, the country's leading soft toy manufacturer. Child's Play implemented a national museum tour featuring Gund's 100-year-old toys, catalogs, and historical photographs. Parents delighted in the sight of Gund toys they had grown up with. Kids loved cuddling contemporary Gunds, making teddy bear pictures, learning about health using teddy bears as their patients—and persuading their moms to buy Gunds in the museum gift shop. In addition to reaching kids and moms directly and generating on-site sales, the event also reached national print and broadcast media, who publicized the event in each city that hosted the exhibit.

# Cause Marketing

MOTHERS CARE ABOUT community. As the number of drive-by shootings and neighborhood crimes increase, mothers have a growing appreciation for raising their children in a safe and nurturing community. They look toward businesses in their community to partner with government agencies to fill the needs of residents. There is a growing loyalty to companies who are rolling up their sleeves and giving back.

Most recently the flame of the volunteerism burned in the wake of September 11, 2001, when Americans generated a renewed sense of patriotism and community support. Being an active participant in the community is an important marketing tool when trying to reach the mom market. Mothers truly appreciate those companies who work with them to make their community better for their children.

A company can get involved in the community in many ways. You can either seek out projects on your own or join a Corporate Volunteer Council (CVC) in your community. CVCs are a group of companies who work together to complete volunteer projects in the community. When I formed the Broward County CVC in 1989 while with the *Miami Herald,* I did so with the help of JM Family Enterprises,

American Express, and Wheelabrator. It was a way for us to work together with our individual employee volunteer programs and make a greater impact on the community.

Our first project was to clean up a park, clearing paths for hiking and refurbishing play areas. Over 200 employees came out early on a Saturday along with their families and helped complete the task at hand. The project received media attention, which gave each company public recognition and free public branding. But the benefits for each participating company didn't stop there. There was a renewed positive attitude among employees who had attended the event. It gave the employees the opportunity to work and socialize together outside the office and accomplish something that gave back to the community, which felt good. That same good feeling went back to the office the following Monday and ultimately translated into increased productivity. The outcome of one weekend of hard work was positive press about the company, improved employee morale, and a new park for the community. From a budget perspective, the event had a great return on investment.

## CASE STUDIES IN EFFECTIVE CAUSE MARKETING

Companies seeking the trust and attention of the mom market have long recognized the power of cause marketing. Cause marketing is defined as tying a marketing message to a particular cause such as cancer, AIDS, literacy, birth defects, or any nonprofit organization. At one time, merely slapping your logo on an event was thought to be sufficient to gain the admiration of consumers. Today's wiser consumers want more from the companies they do business with. Mothers in particular want to know that the companies they are spending money with care about the community. They want to know that these companies are as committed to making the world better for their children as they are. Companies have seen firsthand how those who have demonstrated real commitment to a cause have cashed in on customer loyalty and public awareness.

## McDonald's and Community Ties

McDonald's is a brand synonymous with special event sponsorship and community support for causes. According to Tom Gruber, McDonald's former vice president of International Marketing, McDonald's goal was to sponsor old-fashioned Americana programs, which they ultimately did with the All-American Band program and later the McDonald's All-American Basketball team. Both were far-reaching programs that involved thousands of families from across the United States. "The key is to have a community tie that is altruistic in nature," says Gruber. "The success of the All-American Band program was that it recognized students that had little platform to shine beyond their local community. It also successfully tied-in entire school systems and it had an educational spin. All the components were good. The All-American Band gave McDonald's an opportunity to support students and parents."

Ronald McDonald house is perhaps one of the best known full-scale community projects supported by McDonald's. The project serves the needs of families who have a child receiving long-term health care. Ronald McDonald House Charities makes grants to nonprofit organizations and provides support to Ronald McDonald Houses and Ronald McDonald

Care Mobiles worldwide. To date, Ronald McDonald House Charities' network has awarded more than $300 million to children's programs. (For more information on Ronald McDonald House Charities and its global and local community efforts, visit the RMHC Web site at www.rmhc.org or call 630-623-7048.) What attracts many mothers is that, other than the name, there is no commercialization to it.

## BLOCKBUSTER VIDEO'S KID PRINT PROGRAM

Gruber took his recipe for success from McDonald's and applied it to Blockbuster when he launched the Blockbuster Kid Print Program. The program hit home for mothers because it addressed an issue dear to them—the safety of their child. The program allowed parents to come to a neighborhood Blockbuster store and have their child photographed. Information about the child such as eye and hair color was collected and stored on a passport. In the event that a child was lost or kidnapped the information would be available to law enforcement and media to help recover the child as quickly as possible. The program brought hundreds of thousands of children and their parents into Blockbuster stores.

## AVON'S BREAST CANCER CRUSADE

Avon has created cause marketing success with its crusade on breast cancer. The relationship makes perfect sense since breast cancer attacks the same women that Avon serves. Today the Avon Breast Cancer 3Day event is one of the most attended women's events in the country. The mission of the Avon Breast Cancer Crusade is to fund access to care as well as research to find a cure. Avon's support of the Avon

Breast Cancer Crusade has raised over $165 million in the United States alone since its conception.

# Deciding Which Cause to Support

THERE IS LITTLE argument that companies must be responsible to the communities they serve, but how do you decide which cause to support? Many worthy groups and causes desperately need support in our local communities. The decision is especially difficult when your marketing and philanthropy budget doesn't meet the high demands. Unfortunately, the two will never meet, so your choice must make sense for the company while allowing you the opportunity to showcase your brand.

## Establishing a Charitable Foundation

MANY COMPANIES HAVE established charitable foundations that serve numerous nonprofit organizations on a local and national level. Among them are the Tribune Foundation and Sun-Sentinel Charities, Sara Lee Foundation, and Knight Ridder Foundation. This strategy allows these companies to generate funds through their own efforts and distribute them to causes to which they have ties and commitments. It can be an effective way for larger corporations to manage philanthropic donations.

Causes are getting cluttered with logos and you must find a way to distinguish yourself from the rest of the pack. You don't want to be just another logo on the back of a t-shirt. You also don't want to attach your brand to an event that doesn't make sense for your marketing goals. You don't want to tie yourself to a cause that looks out of the ordinary.

The cause that you choose to support should be relevant to your product's image, speak to your market, or connect you with a desired niche. A baby product company shouldn't select a cause such as colon cancer, when they can associate themselves with a better fit such as March of Dimes. Choose a cause that holds a certain place in the heart of your market. The fear of SIDS or birth defects is certainly closer to the hearts of expectant mothers than colon cancer. If the right event does not exist, you many want to create your own cause special event.

JM Family Enterprises, a billion-dollar diversified automotive company ranked by Forbes as the eighteenth largest privately held company in the United States, did just that when they created the African American Achiever's Awards over a decade ago. The event highlights the accomplishments of African Americans who have made a lasting impression on the lives they've touched. Today the event draws over 1,500 people from the community, attracts media attention, and produces a good feeling among JM Family associates.

# Participating in Events Organized by Others

IF CREATIVITY OR resources restrict you from creating your own special event, how do you select from the thousands of events taking place each year? The two main ways of participating in an event organized by others are: 1) as an event sponsor and 2) buying a booth at a trade fair.

## SPONSORSHIP: CHOOSING WISELY

As the community relations manager for the *Miami Herald,* I used to review over two hundred sponsorship proposals each year. I called one of my criteria "my logo in your hands." After reviewing the proposal, I would ask myself, "How will they handle my logo or brands if I sponsor this event?"

Often I had to look no further than the professionalism of the proposal. If the presentation was haphazardly put together, then I assumed that my logo would be treated in the same manner. I didn't want my company to be attached to an event that didn't serve my customers as I would serve them. Associate yourself only with groups, organizations, and companies that share your business philosophies and marketing goals. For smaller companies, I always recommend selecting partners with the strongest brand in their category or one that already has the attention of your target market. You can't be too careful when selecting your event partners.

The second important aspect of a sponsorship proposal is to consider the benefits you will obtain from your sponsorship. For me while at the *Herald,* hometown exposure was important. Events that could offer exposure such as flyers in schools, posters in local grocery stores, and ads in homeowner newsletters were more valuable than events that gave me expensive advertising minutes with an unqualified audience. Smaller is better when it gives you an opportunity to speak directly to your audience.

Gwen Moran of Moran Marketing offers the following tips to help you spend your sponsorship dollars wisely:

- *Examine the track record.* Look for an event that has been around for several years and is likely to have an established audience. Be sure to get specific details about the average attendance numbers and demographic profiles of attendees. If the event is new, make sure that the producer is reputable and experienced. Many event marketers conduct exit surveys and have other forms of on-site research to better target the event's marketing efforts; see if this information is available for review. The more information you have about the event, the better.

- *Check references.* Once the event organizer has answered your questions, call some of its existing sponsors. Do their descriptions of the attendees match the profiles provided by the event producer? Did the event run smoothly? Find out what they liked—and what they didn't like—about the event, its management, and other functions.

- *Buy a la carte.* Although an event may have existing sponsorship packages, these can often be customized to suit your needs. For instance, a sponsorship package may include 100 free tickets to the event for your customers. If you don't need those tickets, swap them for additional on-site signage or an ad in the event program. Many producers will work to accommodate your needs.

- *Look for promotional opportunities.* Discuss with the event producer how the event will be marketed. You should have access to a list of advertising and marketing vehicles. See if co-op advertising or additional on-site promotional opportunities exist. Can information about your company or a coupon be printed on the back of admission tickets? Can you offer a giveaway to the first 250 people who attend the event?

■ *Be exclusive.* Whatever your business, try to guarantee that you will be the only sponsor of your kind at the event. You will be most effective if you have no on-site competition.

■ *Find out "what if?"* Bad weather or acts of God can spell disaster for an event. Ask what provisions have been made for such situations. Some insurance companies provide event insurance, which protects you if the show does not go on. Also, check with your own insurance agent to make sure that you are adequately covered for any potential liability.

■ *Get it in writing.* Obtain a contract or letter of agreement. Make sure that every detail of your agreement is itemized and that both parties sign the document. Depending on the size of the sponsorship, you may want to show the agreement to your attorney.

## TRADE SHOWS AND EXPOS

Plenty of events offer companies the opportunity to participate without the investment of big-dollar sponsorship. These can be found in fairs, expositions, and other vendor events. Your marketing opportunity usually comes in the form of a booth space. The standard expo area is 10 feet by 10 feet and the rest is up to you.

It can be competitive gaining the attention of mothers when you are one booth in many rows of vendors. When designing your display, consider your strategy for distinguishing yourself from others. Your goal is to get people to stop at your booth and either purchase product or become aware of your goods and services. The visual appearance of your booth should be professional, fun, and attractive. I always recommend some type of activity as well. This might be sampling, drawings for prizes, or games that either the mother or child can play.

One of the best expo booths I ever saw was manned by Funny Bagels. There was always a huge crowd around the booth, which drew more people over to see what all the excitement was about. Funny Bagels had set up a putting green and a ring toss for children, who could play to win a t-shirt. People will do just about anything for a free t-shirt. Next time you are walking through a vendor area, find the booth with the most traffic and I guarantee you they have free t-shirts. They don't even have to be cute or attractive t-shirts, although I suggest designing shirts that fit your marketing plan and portray your brand image. Unfortunately, t-shirts can get expensive and most companies don't have that kind of marketing budget. If you do have the money, the shelf life of a t-shirt is extremely long and will keep selling your brand well after the event.

Drawings are always a good idea for expo booths. They not only attract people to your booth but they give you a mailing list of people who have been introduced to your product. The time that it takes for a person to fill out entry forms is also a good time to pitch your product or service. It gives you a captive audience, which is every marketer's dream.

The down side to vendor booths at fairs and expos is that they tend to be expensive for the amount of exposure you gain. I often hear marketing executives complain that they don't see the results they seek at big expos. A vendor faces many uncontrollable factors such as poor booth location, lower than expected crowds, and lack of buying interest in those who do attend the event.

## CASE STUDY: GO MOM INC.

Molly Gold experienced lackluster results at a baby expo in the early days of Go Mom Inc. The event taught her that sometimes even when all the numbers add up they don't total up to high sales. While working on her business plan, Gold learned about the American Baby Group's Baby Faires. Based on her research regarding high attendance and sponsors like Babies "R" Us and *American Baby* magazine, she concluded that this could be a high-volume sales environment for her product, The GO MOM! Planner.

Unfortunately, Go Mom Inc. underestimated the buying tendencies of the attendees and fell short of projected sales. Although the consumers were largely mothers, they were mostly first-time, younger parents less interested in the time-management benefits that the planner offered.

"After two of these shows," says Gold, "we realized that this was strictly an opportunity for company exposure and networking with fellow vendors. While we did make some great contacts that paid off down the road, lending our young company credibility, without the sales to support the show, it was not a strategy we continued to pursue." Gold's lesson holds value for any marketer. Not only must the numbers add up, but the characteristics of the market must be there as well. I suggest visiting the event you are considering before you actually purchase your booth space. Apply the market research method I described at the beginning of this book: people-watch. Are mothers pushing strollers past every booth without stopping? Are they too busy with their children to listen to sales pitches or to watch wonderful product videos? Are they stopping at a booth to play games, fill out contest entries, or pick up samples? Look around and see which brands are the most visible. It might be the company handing out big plastic bags with their logo on them. Bags are great giveaway items at events for mothers, especially when they are collecting lots of freebies. Investing a little time beforehand may save you from wasting a lot of money later.

■  ■  ■

Whether it's a fair, festival, parade, expo, or lecture, special events offer a great way to get out and touch moms. It's valuable time spent listening to her concerns, gaining her feedback, and introducing her to the faces behind your company. With careful selection and well-conceived execution, event sponsorship can succeed in telling mom what's special about your company. Showing that you care about the community in which she is raising her children is an old-fashioned message that has suddenly become quite important again.

## CHAPTER NINE

# Marketing to Moms Through Their Children

N O MATTER WHERE you live in the United States, the scene is the same. A mother pushes a bright red cart through a Target store while her toddler sits in the buggy seat and her school-aged child strolls slowly behind, sneaking a touch of every single item that is stacked on the low shelf of an end-aisle display. When his mother turns to instruct him to hurry along, the toddler takes advantage of the stopped cart and grabs a Matchbox car off a display. "But mom, can't I just get one thing?" the child says in a drawn-out whine that he accents by throwing his shoulders forward and dragging his feet. The mother turns back to her cart to find six new items inside, compliments of an eager toddler enticed by brightly colored boxes. The scenario will be repeated as least three more times within a 10-minute window. There is a high probability that before exiting the store, mom will voice the words all marketers love to hear, "Okay, you can get it."

At the other end of the mall, a mother with her nine-year-old daughter shops the racks at Old Navy. The daughter holds up the latest style of low-rider jeans while her mother silently wishes that little pink dresses were the object of her desire. She suggests a more conservative pair of khakis, which receive a quick veto. The shopping experience continues in the same manner until careful negotiations take place in the dressing room. Mom will buy the khakis and allow her daughter to spend her allowance on the low riders. The pink dress remains a pipe dream.

Just as our visit to a park at the beginning of this book gave us a firsthand view of the spending power of mothers, a walk in the mall can give us a glimpse into the influence a mother's children have over her spending. It should come as no surprise that the buying power of a mother extends beyond her own wallet and into the pockets of her children. Marketers have been wise to this fact for years and focused their efforts not only on mom but on her children as well. The goal of savvy advertisers is to capture the attention of children and leverage their influence over their mothers to increase sales. This ripple effect of influence and spending contributes to the value marketers realize in the mom market. The combination of persuasive advertising and what is known as the "nag factor" (a child's expressive desire for a product), creates a marketing strategy that is difficult for a mother to avoid.

Marketing through a mother's toddlers, tweens, and teens is an effective way to capture the buying power of the mom market. It is a successful marketing strategy because it can be used with any stage of mother, playing to a mother's desire to make her children happy. All mothers want to please their children. Moms aspire to give their children more than they had as children themselves. Today the definition of "more" tends to take the form of material things, from family vacations to the latest computer to the newest style of Nike shoes.

In addition, the pop-culture marketplace has created an arena that is associated with a child's self-esteem and peer acceptance. The fear of creating a playground outcast or teen loner because of the absence of the latest acceptable fashion logo is too great a burden for a mother to bear.

The final reason that marketing to moms through their children works emerges from mothers' recent desire for balance in their busy lives. Fighting with a straight-A teen over the brand of jeans can waste precious time and energy. Instead, a mother may concede to letting her wear the type of jeans she wants as long as her grades remain high.

Marketing to children is a controversial subject that can spark long debates on whether it is right to exploit the power children have over their parents, whether it is healthy to integrate so many marketing messages into the classroom, or whether advertisers should lure children into sharing personal data. Not all moms like the attempts to market through their children. Marketing to children has been blamed for everything from violence to obesity in children.

Some believe that slogans such as "You deserve a break today," "Have it your way," "Obey your thirst," and "Just do it," speak to getting what you want and getting it now, not desirable characteristics to encourage in children. As a mother, I can appreciate the defenseless feeling marketers create by consulting with psychologists when creating their marketing strategies. As a marketing professional, however, I can appreciate the desire of companies to create strategies to maximize the return on their marketing initiatives. We are not going to debate these issues. It is a reality that advertisers speak to mothers through their children. It is a subject that could fill many a book by itself. I won't attempt to detail all the elements of this complex subject but rather will give you enough information about child marketing to allow you to appreciate its impact on the mom market.

# The Enormity of the Child Market

MAKE NO MISTAKE about it, the child market offers advertisers an incredible opportunity. In size alone it offers a desirable market. According to the 2000 Census, there are 80 million Americans under the age of eighteen, and 39 million kids ages five to fourteen.[1] Households with school-age children outspend households without children by at least one-third.[2]

Like any desirable market, the child market can make an impact to the bottom line of companies who tap into it. A study released by the Kaiser Family Foundation estimates that children directly control $24.4 billion in spending and influence another $300 billion a year in purchases.[3] Topping the list of powerhouse spenders are tweens (children between the ages of eight and fourteen), who spend close to $14 billion a year and influence more than $128 billion in family-food purchases alone. Teens aren't doing too shabbily themselves. The nation's 23 million teenagers eat, on average, 4.33 times each day, 365 days a year. That is a lot of Bagel Bites, cereal, French fries, and Coca-Cola. It's no wonder that beverage companies are willing to pay top dollar to lure stars such as Britney Spears to sing the praises of their drinks.

# The Potential for Lifelong Customers

MARKETERS ARE ATTRACTED to the child market because it offers the opportunity to gain "a customer for life." Many child marketers call it the "cradle to grave" market. They win the child's admiration when he can influence his parent's buying decisions; later he becomes a customer when he is spending his own money and purchasing for his own family. Unfortunately, many companies who see children as potential customers for life forget to incorporate retention programs later in the life of the consumer. Smart companies will realize that, unlike Peter Pan, children grow up and they must refocus their marketing efforts to reward customer loyalty and retain valuable consumers.

Marketing to children is not a new concept. A short walk down memory lane might take you to a metal lunch box adorned with Spiderman, the Brady Bunch, or the Hulk. Companies have used characters to attract attention to their product since the turn of the century. Buster Brown, the Campbell's Soup Kids, and the Blockbuster Kids are just a few of the fictitious identities that have come to life on radio and television, compliments of advertisers.

# Where Marketers Find Children

CHILDREN HAVE PLENTY of time to hear the messages of advertisers. According to the Kaiser Family Foundation, American children spend an average of nearly 40 hours a week consuming television or radio outside of school.[4] This is almost equal to the time their parents spend at a full-time job. Children watch 50 to 100 television commercials per day. That's 20,000 to 40,000 television ads annually.

Children are also getting advertising messages online. According to the Center for Media Education, a national nonprofit organization dedicated to creating quality electronic media culture for children and the initiator of the Chilren's Online Privacy Protection Act (COPPA), nearly three-quarters of twelve to seventeen year olds are online.[5] They surpass adults in their use of chat, instant messaging, and other forms of Internet communications. They are also more likely to click on banner ads. This same group has a total annual spending power of $8.9 billion, according to *Brandweek* magazine.[6]

For this reason, it is important for marketers to know where teens are congregating on the Web. According to the Center for Media Education report, teens are heading to entertainment online, visiting sites such as MamaMedia.com, Bolt.com, and Alloy.com where they can find music, advice, chat, free e-mail, fashion news, and virtual pen pals. Advertisers are partnering with these sites to create branded destinations, such as Cover Girl who sponsors the CG Connection Club as a way to appeal to teens. For advertisers, it's not only branding that they gain online with teens but sales as well. The median amount of money Web users ages thirteen to fifteen spend online per year is $360. It rises to $540 for ages sixteen to seventeen.[7]

Marketers, whether or not for the good of the family unit, are doing a good job of penetrating the minds and attitudes of children. By the age of three, before they can even read, children are making brand-name requests. The Center for a New American Dream reports that a six-month-old baby begins to formalize images of corporate logos and product at the same time they are beginning to crawl and make babbling noises.[8]

# Case Studies: Speaking Effectively to Children (and Their Moms)

YOU DON'T HAVE to look hard to find companies who speak to mothers by targeting their children. You'll find them as close as your neighborhood golden arches and in your morning bowl of oatmeal. Companies know that mothers listen to their children and want to make them happy. Several brand's messages can be heard louder and more effectively than others. Let's look at those who do a good job getting their marketing messages delivered to mother by children.

## McDonald's: A Leader in Marketing to Children

McDonald's spends over $550 million a year on advertising to successfully reach children and families. Their earliest marketing dollars were used to purchase advertising during children's programming. According to Tom Gruber, former vice president of International Marketing for McDonald's, since many of those shows were cartoons, McDonald's decided to use Ronald McDonald, a cartoon character.

"They (children) were watching cartoons so our commercials were cartoon characters. The commercials were designed to be a step up from the shows that children were watching in order to be acceptable to mothers. Advertisers have to pay attention to what they want their children to see and watch," says Gruber, the father of two girls. "McDonald's had two distinct and separate campaign focuses; adults and children. They use their child marketing to speak to mothers through their children. McDonald's realizes that without the awareness of the mothers, children have no access to their products."

One of the strongest marketing initiatives for McDonald's was the implementation of play centers. Suddenly children wanted to go to McDonald's not only to eat the hamburgers and French fries but also for the experience of playing on the playgrounds. Eating at McDonald's became an outing and a positive experience. But mothers also applauded the addition. The play centers were a solution to a challenge shared by almost every mother: how to keep your child busy and active.

In an effort to continue to transform moms into "fast feeders" even as their children get older, they introduced the Mighty Kids Meal in 2001. The new meal, which is a super-sized version of their popular Happy Meal, is designed to reflect the interests of children ages eight to ten.

To ensure a connection with mothers, McDonald's launched humorous Mighty Kids ads featuring mothers dealing with the awkward stage that occurs when their children leave the preschool but before they become teens. The ads allow mothers to laugh at themselves, and they offer a fast dining solution and a way for moms to stay connected to the fond memories they have of sharing Happy Meals with their children. McDonald's plays off the success they had in building a memorable experience for moms and their children when they created play dates that included a Happy Meal and time at a McDonald's play center.

## Lego's Partnership Strategy

Some brands partner together in order to reach the level of success that McDonald's has in connecting with children and mothers. Lego illustrated its continued appreciation for the symbiotic relationship between the consumer influence of children and the buying power of their mothers by partnering with Quaker Oats. In the 2001 back-to-school season, Lego Studios partnered with Quaker Oats in their "Fun in a bowl" campaign. In an effort to promote its newest oatmeal product, Treasure Hunt Instant Oatmeal, Quaker Oats targeted children ages six to nine with national TV ads, print ads, sampling efforts, and promotions with Lego. In addition, print ads aimed at moms were run in women's titles.

The new oatmeal (which includes sugar treasure chests that melt into green, red, and gold coins when hot water is added) were a perfect tie-in to Lego's Moviemaker line because Lego moviemaker has treasure-seeking characters in its sets. An on-pack promotion with Lego offers fun that starts at the breakfast table and continues when you are playing with your new Lego set. The initiative went beyond traditional advertising by distributing more than 3 million samples with discounted coupons to parents at school open-houses and PTA programs. This was not the first time Lego aimed its marketing guns at children and mothers. For the past two years, Lego has initiated a holiday campaign that targets three consumer groups: Lego enthusiasts, mothers, and of course, children under twelve. In a rich media campaign that included banners, buttons, and mini-sites (specially branded Web pages within a Web site), Lego placed ads on popular female sites such as About.com as well as sites mothers and children visit together, such as NickJr.com and Disney.com.

## A RETAIL STRATEGY: PLAY AREAS AND KIDS' SECTIONS

Tom Gruber applied his McDonald's play-area experience to help Blockbuster Video tap the mom market by adding kids' sections to all its stores. "The play areas included themed rugs, activities, and later the Blockbuster Kids, two oversized, cartoon-like characters with an oversized smile and real-life like look and feel," says Gruber. "Initially our marketing targeted the adult in the family because it was the adult, and in most cases, the mother who had to transport the child to our store. But once the family got to the store, we wanted mothers to know that there was a safe, fun area for their child to hang out while they selected their video."

Gruber also used this family-friendly strategy at Auto-Nation. "Our idea was to create a safe, fun area within the store to drop off your children while you browsed the car selection, had your vehicle serviced, or took delivery of your new car," explains Gruber.

The play centers were large, colorful areas outfitted with giant climbing sets, videos, and art activities. Each center was supervised by a childcare professional and strict safety measures were incorporated to ensure that children would be safe. It became a real point of differentiation in the car industry. There were no other automobile retailers who created a child-friendly buying experience. "Parents loved it," says Gruber.

Customer loyalty is greater when based upon a unique shopping experience. Providing a safe, wholesome solution to keeping her child occupied is something every mom is looking for in her day.

## HOLIDAY INN: DESIGNING A PRODUCT FOR MOMS AND KIDS

According to Terry Whaples of Holiday Inn Family Suites, when Holiday Inn was designing this new product, it asked moms and kids what they wanted in a hotel and took the time to really listen to their answers. It wasn't enough to just print "Kids Eat Free" in the brochures. Says Whaples, "We had to have foods that kids genuinely liked. We sat with families and walked the dining room to find out what foods children wanted and then gave it to their value-conscious mothers for free. We appeal to our littlest customers because we treat children like people. As a mom myself, if my kids receive VIP treatment and have a good time, then I'm happy, too. My entire team took an oath when we launched the Family Suites that we would childrenize the travel experience in order to appeal to kids."

Holiday Inn Family Suites serve drinks in plastic cups with lids and make it clear that it's okay if a child cries in the dining room, which not only makes it less stressful for the child but for the mom as well. In addition, rooms are childproofed with electrical socket plugs and mothers are offered complimentary child-proofing kits that include baby monitors and bath water thermometers at check-in.

But it's not only the moms who receive safety gear. "Children enjoy watching a safety video featuring my puppet, Daisy," says Whaples. "By the time the family leaves, we are confident that not only the mother is talking about her good time but her children are as well. We've been successful in building a tremendous amount of loyalty. We know that children tell their friends about us."

## Funny Bagels

Rarely have I seen a new product enter the consumer market with as much proficiency in tapping both the mom and child market as Funny Bagels, a prepackaged lunch alternative to

Lunchables. A Funny Bagel is a shaped like a smile, pre-sliced to make a sandwich, and comes packaged with health-ful complements such as yogurt and apple juice.

Funny Bagels runs two sets of television commercials. One targets moms and carries descriptions such as: "Mom solves the dilemma of what to feed the kids for lunch and feels good about it," and "Mom shows just how fast and sim-ple a Funny Bagels On-The-Go Combo can be." These two messages speak to the time-starved mother. Their other set of ads speak to kids by using football players and the theme of thinking big and having fun while eating Funny Bagels.

Funny Bagels reinforces both messages on its Web site, www.funnybagels.com, by offering moms nutritional infor-mation and kids online games.

■ ■ ■

As companies rewrite their marketing plans to include the child market, it is important for them to find the right mix of messages that will speak to both the mother and the child in a language they understand. Success will be achieved by being "cool" or "tight" and attractive to their mothers at the same time.

## Using Kick-Butt Femininity

Bruce Tait of Fallon Brand Consulting faced a similar chal-lenge with a blue-jean client. Tait's goal was to gain the ap-proval of the end-user, the tween, and the consumer, her mother. "It was important to win over the tween but make sure that we weren't turning off moms. It was crucial that we put any worries of sleazy to rest with the mothers of our tween target market."

To learn how they could manage this relationship, Tait held focus groups with kids and mothers. First, the tweens and their mothers were in separate focus groups and then they were put together. Says Tait, "We discovered that the tweens changed the way they talked in the presence of their mothers. We learned that they persuade their mothers in a variety of ways. First, it is the 'I'll wear them a lot,' appealing to mothers who hate to buy something only to have their children never wear it. Second, it's the 'everybody's got them. I don't want to be a loser in school.' This gets the parent thinking, 'do I want them to be the one standing out in the crowd?' so the tactic works."

Ultimately, Tait says, they developed product, packaging, and merchandising materials that primarily appealed to the tweens, but stayed safely inside the parameters of parental acceptability. "We found that there was a 'kick-butt femininity' strategy that was appealing to both moms who felt jeans could be empowering and not overtly adult sexy and tween girls who felt they were reminiscent of cool movies like *Charlie's Angels*."

## MAKING HEALTHFUL APPEALING TO KIDS

Yogurt, once perceived as a health and diet food for older women, has joined the effort to focus on youth as well as their mothers. The introduction of kid-friendly flavors and product lines such as Trix yogurt and Danimals has done a lot to increase sales in recent years. Dannon not only launched Danimals but also made it fun for children to consume their product by making it drinkable.

In 1999, Dannon switched their marketing efforts from moms to focus on kids. In previous branding efforts, Danimals yogurt had been pitched to moms as a healthful kids' snack with no artificial colors or flavors. The thought was exciting for moms but not their children. Dannon's new goal is to build recognition of four cartoon animal characters—a polar bear, a dinosaur, a monkey, and a brown bear—which are featured on the packaging. Creating a brand that attracts kids pleases moms as well by eliminating the nagging that goes with getting kids to eat a healthful snack like yogurt. Dannon's campaign included fun commercials, bright packaging, and in-store displays and has been successful in capturing additional sales.

## KID MAGAZINES

*Time, Sports Illustrated,* and *People* are just a few of the magazine titles that have a child version available to the offspring of their subscribers: *Time for Kids, Sports Illustrated for Kids,* and *Teen People.* They successfully attract both moms and youngsters to their publications. The mother sees her subscription as not only access to leisure reading for herself but also as a solution to her desire to enrich her child through reading. *Time for Kids* takes the big stuff and puts it in terms that are easy to understand and palatable to both parent and child. The best part for moms is that it is free of advertising. The effort speaks to a mother's desire to fuel her child's interest in reading and learning. Today's mothers are convinced that reading holds the key to the academic success of their children. Well-conceived initiatives such as these are not only breeding future readers and subscribers but also creating consumer loyalty in their parents. A wonderful example of integrating a retention effort into "cradle to grave" marketing, this strategy could produce bottom-line results for your company.

▪ ▪ ▪

As we have seen in prior chapters, there are multitudes of ways to speak to the mom market. Although there is strong debate over the acceptability of marketing to children, one thing is certain, the influence of children on mom's buying decisions is undeniable. Moms listen to the needs and desires of their children and react by spending money on your products and services. By integrating marketing messages and efforts that appeal to both the mother and her child, you, too, can gain your piece of the billion of dollars of purchasing decisions they will make together.

## CHAPTER TEN

# Using Public Relations to Reach Moms

NOTHING DRIVES SALES up and gets moms talking about your company like a good public relations story. The old adage about the power of the press is true, and the word-of-mom buzz it can create is even more powerful. The list of businesses that have grown out of one good newspaper article or five minutes on "Good Morning America" is long. Think about the Rubik cube, Baby Einstein videos, or any of the Oprah Book Club titles. The best thing about good press is that it most often comes with a small price tag. A single well-written press release can spawn an avalanche of media attention. One rule to remember is that the press is no different than anyone else; if others have it, they want it. Your challenge is to create a media buzz about your product and gain their attention.

## The Media As a Customer

THERE ARE SEVERAL tricks to rising above the tall pile of press releases received by newsrooms each day. The first is to treat members of the media as customers. That means respond quickly to their needs, deliver the best product possible, maintain a good relationship, research your market, and respect their time. Just as you would target the right customer for your business, it's important to focus your efforts on the correct reporters for your story. During my career at the *Miami Herald*, people would send us letters addressed to another newspaper or to writers who no longer wrote for us.

Spend a day familiarizing yourself with reporters who cover stories like the one you plan to present. Keep in mind the interests of the moms you want to target and consider the sections of the paper they read. Each news organization may have more than one area to consider. For example, when we launched BlueSuitMom.com, we sent materials to the technology writer, local business writer, and lifestyle editor. To gain additional exposure, we even sent personnel-appointment announcements to the business section because we knew that the executive mothers we were targeting read the business-promotions listings. Take any mention you can get, even if it's just in the personnel or new businesses column.

## THE NEEDS OF YOUR CUSTOMER

Keep in mind the needs of your customer, in this case a reporter looking for a story. The product you need to deliver is a unique story with an interesting angle. A good story idea can make all the difference in whether you gain a two-sentence mention in a column or a feature story on the cover of the family living section. A simple "We are proud to announce our new product designed for mothers" just won't do it. What makes your product unique? Why would a mother find it interesting and what does it offer that she can't find somewhere else?

Think about what makes you read an article in the newspaper or stop to watch a news segment. Personal stories, heroic efforts, first-of-its kind products, or providing a solution to a commonly known problem are all good places to look for an angle. We launched BlueSuitMom.com with several press releases that included several different messages. Below are the headlines to each:

BLUESUITMOM.COM LAUNCHES FIRST WEB
SITE TARGETING EXECUTIVE MOTHERS

FIRST WOMEN'S SITE TO OFFER VIRTUAL CLASSES
LAUNCHES ON MOTHER'S DAY

LOCAL MOM MARRIES PERSONAL LIFE
WITH BUSINESS

In the first press release, we identified ourselves as the first to market to a unique niche. In the second, we focused on what set us apart from other women's sites, virtual classes. The third presented a local flare to the story. Although some reporters received all releases, each release went only to the appropriate writers.

## THE RIGHT STORY ANGLE

Finding the right story angle can be perfected with experience.

### Determine Your Goal

The first step is to decide on the goal of the publicity you are seeking. What do you want to accomplish? What are your goals? Is it a feature story, inclusion in a special working-mother section, or a listing in top toys for Christmas?

Susan Harrow, founder of Harrow Communications and author of *Sell Yourself Without Selling Your Soul: A Woman's Guide to Promoting Herself, Her Business, or Her Cause with Integrity and Spirit* (HarperCollins, 2002), agrees that setting goals is an important first step in initiating a successful public relations effort. "The number one mistake most publicists make is they don't focus on their goals. News seekers will say, 'I want to get PR in the *New York Times*' without understanding what types of clients they want to obtain or the qualities those customers will possess. Public relations efforts should be planned to bring in the right customers."

Harrow recently worked with a company of career counselors who wrote articles as a way to gain publicity for their services. Although they had managed to get the articles into several newspapers, they were dissatisfied with their results. Harrow reviewed their articles and noticed that the writer used lawyers as examples of people using their services—yet in reality the career counselors didn't want lawyers for clients. "We immediately changed the articles to show the customers they were targeting. Your audience should see themselves in your product," says Harrow. "You also want your philosophy and ethics to be subtly communicated as well by demonstrating that everything in your company is in alignment with what you want to promote. To appeal to moms, use stories that have strong emotional resonance or stories about how dangerous situations can be avoided. Motherhood brings on the extra-protective hormone so moms have heightened awareness of things that could possibly endanger their child, family, home, job, security," advises Harrow.

## Step into Their Shoes

Wearing the shoes of a reporter allows us to look at what's being picked up currently in the media. Examine the trends and topics that reporters are finding timely. Is there something that we can expand on to give our reporter a new way of telling an old story?

Working for Stork Avenue last year, BSM Media wanted to release the most popular names of 2001 but knew that others were also releasing similar information to the press. So instead of simply announcing that Michael, Jacob, and Emily were the most common names of the year, we created a public relations strategy in which Stork Avenue released a list of names it projected to be popular in 2002. By using the database of names and popularity it had from the past decade and applying trending data, voilà, the company had a new story to present to the media. The release resulted in stories about Stork Avenue's baby-name predictions appearing in *Parent's* magazine, *Today's Parent* newspaper, the *Salt Lake City Tribune,* and several others.

## Look at Solutions and Trends

When trying to find the right story to attract the mom market, ask yourself if you solve a problem for mothers in some unique or unusual way. Another way to find a story is to look at your market in terms of what you know about them. Is there a recent trend you have noticed, like more money being spent on a particular widget you sell and if so, why? A story about record sales of a particular item because of a baby boom in your area is not only newsworthy but creates a buzz among mothers who think that if other moms need it, then they do, too.

## Using Special Events

Sometimes finding a unique angle or story might necessitate creating a special event, promotion, survey, or contest to attract attention to your product. As we learned in the last chapter, a properly targeted and planned special event can do

# Using the Retail Calendar for Story Ideas

GWEN MORAN OF Moran Marketing Associates offers this creative suggestion for getting the attention of the press. "Use the retail calendar as a promotional tool. For many consumer-oriented businesses, the calendar that reads 'January, February, March . . .' is not nearly as important as the one that reads, 'Martin Luther King Jr. Day, Valentine's Day, Presidents Day' and so on."

The retail calendar can offer opportunities for many businesses to create innovative and effective promotions. For example, Nathan's Famous, the renowned hot-dog maker, holds an international hot-dog eating contest on Coney Island each Independence Day. The wiener master hosts entrants from around the world in the fight for the title of International Hot Dog Eating Champion.

If you're tired of the same old celebrations, check out Chase's Calendar of Events (www.chases.com). This comprehensive listing contains more than 12,000 entries including celebrity birthdays, astrological phenomena, culinary celebrations, and festivals around the world, fully indexed by location, date, and category.

wonders for attracting the positive attention of moms. Look at your audience and available resources to determine what is relevant to your company yet interesting to the media.

### Tapping into a Unique Client Base

There might be something unique about your client base. In the case of BlueSuitMom.com, we have a large audience of executive working mothers. We often poll them about their attitudes related to timely news issues and offer the results to members of the press as a means for them to broaden the scope of their stories. For instance, last year we anticipated that newspapers would be writing stories about Mother's Day gifts so we polled our readers on what working mothers desired from their families for Mother's Day and offered the results to writers to supplement articles they already had planned. As a result, we not only enjoyed national print exposure but also were featured on a CBS affiliate in the Chicago market. The effort certainly paid for itself.

## CREATING MEDIA EVENTS

Many companies have successfully created their own events to gain the attention of the media and the mom market. Crayola has launched several "name the new color" contests, which earned them spots on many daytime news shows. Currently Heinz is seeking suggestions for names and colors of future ketchups. By allowing consumers to create their own cereal online, General Mills has earned offline publicity for their efforts.

In 1995, Sure Fit, a slipcover company, launched the Ugliest Couch Contest, a promotion that invited the public to submit photos of their outdated or worn-out couches. The promotion made perfect sense for a company whose product offers homeowners easy decorating solutions. The contest generated thousands of entries and the best part was that anyone who owned an ugly couch was a potential client for a Sure Fit slipcover.

In addition, the contest attracted the attention of the media. It was a unique and humorous story idea that had a somewhat longer shelf life than many time-sensitive stories. The contest also offered a before, during, and after opportunity for publicity, which kept Sure Fit in the media for an extended amount of time. For the grand finale to a superb public relations effort, Sure Fit arranged to have the winner announced on "Live with Regis and Kelly."

## EDUCATE YOURSELF

In addition to creating your own stories, it is helpful to know what stories reporters are writing. Once you could only access this information if you were fortunate enough to have well-established relationships with reporters, but the Internet has created new forms of communications for publicists and writers. Services, such as Profnet, list queries submitted by reporters. Each day, you can receive lists of summaries from writers looking for sources for stories they are working on currently. This timesaving tool is worth the annual fee for companies who are seeking media attention. Profnet also allows companies to submit story ideas, which are then sent out to a database of journalists in a leads newsletter. This service allows you to put your creative story ideas in front of thousands of writers each week.

# Positioning Yourself with the Press

SEASONED PUBLIC RELATIONS executives will tell you that their relationship with members of the press is their most valuable asset. Keep in mind that reporters need stories and if you bring them a good story, you have made their job easier. Develop a good reputation with reporters by positioning yourself as a resource for future stories. Make it known that you are available to them with a list of industry contacts or statistics, even if you aren't included in the article. I always offer additional angles to every story I pitch. I also provide names and contact information for other people who can be a part of the story, even if they're competitors. The practice allows me to exhibit the type of objectivity that journalists admire and respect.

Another way to earn the respect of reporters is to position yourself or members of your company as experts. If an area of expertise doesn't seem obvious, look at the solutions that your product or company offers to the mom market. For instance, Molly Gold, creator of the Go Mom planner, has established herself as an expert in the area of busy mom scheduling because her planner helps moms organize their family's schedules and activities. This role earned her a spot on "Good Morning America" as an expert coaching busy moms.

You can take the first step to establishing your credibility and expertise by getting published in your area of interest. The Internet offers plenty of opportunities to become published. Simply write a few articles and distribute them as free content to relevant sites that serve your market and potential customers. Karen Deerwester, a parenting coach, not only expands her professional resume by serving as an expert on

## Pitching a Story

WHEN YOUR RELATIONSHIP with a reporter requires you to pitch a story, Susan Harrow provides these tips, "I coach my clients to act like a mother when they are pitching a story. How would you tell a story to your child? How do you communicate to your family? The reason I use this example is because we speak more freely to our children and we tend to tell a story in a way that even a child can understand. Try to come up with the most emotionally powerful story. Practice in speaking in sound bites by running your story by a teenager. They can sniff out anything fake or boring. Media will respond much like a teenager."

BlueSuitMom.com but also positions herself as a national resource for writers looking for comments on early childhood development. In a large company, you have the opportunity to position several people with varied areas of expertise, thus creating multiple channels of communication between you and the media.

## Press Kits

SOMETIMES EVEN WITH good relationships and an interesting story, you need to rise above the clutter to get noticed by the media. I can easily credit the early success of

BlueSuitMom.com to our initial public relations efforts. To get noticed, we created a unique press kit. We decided to launch our company on Mother's Day in order to capitalize on the established media interest in mothers during the month of May. Attaching yourself to Mother's Day comes with risks even if you are a mother-driven business because the media is literally bombarded with Mother's Day-themed press releases.

The press kits were designed to look like an expensive Mother's Day gift.

I call it the "Tiffany's blue box" approach to public relations. Although our press kits were assembled on the office floor, we wanted them to look representative of a larger company. They were made out of oversized glossy white boxes, large enough for several unfolded press releases and promotional items. We created large gift tags on our office computers, which read: "On Mother's Day, 11 million mothers will receive the same gift." Notice how we immediately positioned the magnitude of our market and created a sense of curiosity.

When the recipient opened the box, they found neatly creased blue tissue paper with the answer: "BlueSuitMom .com" was taped across the fold of the paper just as an expensive department store might wrap a package. Included in the box were not only press releases and the bios of our management team but promotional items designed for busy executive mothers. We included a school note pad, pen, small box of crayons, and a chocolate bar. Each one was imprinted with our logo. Our tactical approach was that even if they didn't read our releases, who can resist using free stuff or eating chocolate? The chocolate bars were wrapped in specially designed wrappers that listed the ingredients of our site, the name "BlueSuitMom.com" in bold letters, and contact information. We knew that our name was catchy and if they took a minute to go to our site, we were confident they would find a great product.

Our media list was strategically planned to include mainly female members of the press. This selective process gave us a good chance of landing our press kit in the hands of a working mother, which would mean that our press materials would be read by someone who herself was our market and could relate to our information. Winning the heart of a mother is important but if she happens to be a mother and a member of the media, it's even better.

Within the first week of launching our site, BlueSuit Mom.com was in the *Fort Lauderdale Sun Sentinel, Philadelphia Inquirer, Denver Post, Salt Lake City Tribune,* and *Lincoln Journal Star.* Within a month, we were featured in over twenty print publications including the *Wall Street Journal* and *USA Today* and three electronic news segments. The most startling thing was that the entire initial effort, including overnighting the packages, cost only $1,800. We could not have bought advertising that would have produced as much traffic for the same money.

In light of September 11 and the anthrax episodes that followed, I would apply additional considerations to sending press kits and food items to the media. Remember that newsrooms are taking additional precautions and applying new standards when opening boxes. Do not send anything to a news organization without clearly labeling a return address on the outside. Send it by a traceable delivery service to establish an additional level of trust with the reporter.

Eye-catching photos that help the reporter visualize your story will help you gain media attention. Media professionals like knowing that good visuals are available. Don't send head shots except to business columnists. Instead arrange to have action shots. When we were launching "Mom Talk Radio" for the Chris Evert Children's Hospital, we mailed slick press folders, which included a picture of a young child at the microphone in the radio studio. A dialogue box above the picture said, "There's a new voice on radio in South Florida." It's difficult to resist a picture of a cute kid and the copy enticed reporters to read on. This campaign resulted in articles in the *Miami Herald, Sun Sentinel, South Florida Parenting* magazine, *Women's Day,* and *SELF.*

# Press Releases

THE FINAL STEP to gaining media attention is to present a well-written press release. What seems like the most obvious step is often ignored. Don't forget to include contact information, business location, and other important facts. There are industry-recognized standards to follow when drafting your press releases. It may seem elementary, but be sure to include the five Ws in the first paragraph: who, what, when, where, and why. A good quote in the body of the press release, supporting statistics, and crediting the source are important elements. The final paragraph should be a boilerplate description of your business that clearly and quickly tells the reader who you are.

Many services are available to help you distribute your press releases. If you decide to hire a public relations firm, they should have established relationships with these organizations. But you don't have to be a public relations professional to gain access to these services.

# Rules of Writing and Distributing Press Releases

- Include contact information, name, phone number, and e-mail at the top.
- Include a release date if the information is time-sensitive. FOR IMMEDIATE RELEASE is appropriate if you do not want the reader to hold the story.
- Type the HEADLINE in all caps to gain the attention of the reader.
- Use an italicized subheading to present an additional story angle or highlight the uniqueness of your news.
- Include who, what, where, when, and why in the first paragraph. Keep it short and concise.
- Use good grammar and spelling.
- Limit your release to one page.
- Include a boilerplate at the bottom of the press release.
- End the release with the word "End" or "###."
- Never send a release as an attachment. Paste the copy into the body of the e-mail.
- Never fax a press release unless you follow it up with a short phone call.
- Attach only black-and-white photos.

PRNewswire distributes news releases and photos to the media. Other companies that offer distribution services include Business Wire, www.businesswire.com; Internet Wire, www.internetwire.com; Xpress Press, www.xpress.com.

# Television PR

So you want to be on television? Gaining the attention of television media can present different challenges but is a great way to reach a large number of mothers quickly. If you believe you have a product or story that belongs on "Today" or one of its competitors, it's essential that your research be thorough. Stephanie Azzarone of Child's Play shares her expertise in winning the hearts of television producers:

- *News clues.* See a segment that relates to your company? Find out who produced it and get in touch.
- *Net-working.* Use Web sites to research when similar stories last appeared, who was responsible for them, what approach was taken, and more.
- *Special interests.* Talk shows often have regular segments focused on a particular topic, such as parenting or new products. Find out what they are, who presents them, who produces them, and when they air.
- *Picture this.* Think visually. For all of you dealing with kids' products and services, the best visual is kids.
- *A good read.* TV gets many of its ideas from the newspapers, so get print coverage first.
- *Keep on calling.* As every publicist knows, there's a fine line between being persistent and being a Pain. But given the alternative—no story—opt for the big P, but do it with style.

## "Oprah"

When people think moms and television, "Oprah" is the word. Susan Harrow, the author of *How to Get on Oprah* (www .prsecretstore.com/ultimateguide.html), agrees that there is an

undeniable desire by experts, authors, and product manufacturers to land a spot in front of the millions of women
who watch "Oprah."

"People believe that getting on 'Oprah' will make them a
millionaire, their book a bestseller, or their business boom.
For your career to take off like the last space shuttle, you
must prepare to make the most of your appearance," says
Harrow. As a media coach and marketing expert, Harrow
has helped many people get booked on "Oprah." She offers
the following hot tips to help you get invited as a guest on
the show, rivet your audience on the air, and ultimately sell
yourself along with your product:

1.  Record two to four weeks of "Oprah." Then, sit down in
    a comfy spot and watch them all at once. This will give
    you a sense of what's hot on "Oprah" for the next few
    months. Notice which producers (listed on the credits at
    the end) are responsible for each particular type of seg-
    ment. Send a producer information only after you are
    sure of whom you'd like to approach and why.
2.  Pitch a hot topic. Never pitch yourself, your speech, or
    your product. Instead pitch something that's newswor-
    thy: a pressing national issue, a controversial subject, a
    problem for which you have the solution, a common
    myth debunked. Propose a topic that is relevant to Win-
    frey's audience (controversy, relationships, personal tri-
    umph, makeovers), then prove you are the expert by
    telling only the information that is relevant to the idea
    you're pitching.
3.  Put together a winning press package. Include a copy of
    your book or product with a pitch or angle page with two
    or three different ideas; also include a paragraph bio

highlighting your expertise as it pertains to your pitches. Be brief. You must be able to sell your idea in one page. Remember "Oprah" producers get hundreds of packages every day. If possible include a two-to-four-minute video of you on other talk shows or doing a presentation to a group. If your demo video includes talk show clips, cue it up to those segments. If not, cue your video up to a short segment that shows you speaking succinctly so the producers can see that you're a viable guest.

4. Explore the show's Web site. Winfrey's Web site, www .oprah.com, has as much information as you will ever need to get on the show. There, you can review her entire wish list of subjects. She even makes it easy for you with a link called "Be on the show." With the touch of a key you can send an e-mail that will reach her producers instantly.

   Let the producers know that you'd be glad to hop a red-eye at a moment's notice to be a part of their show, and you increase your chances of being invited.

5. Create six dynamic sound bites. Mark Twain defines a sound bite as "a minimum of sound to a maximum of sense." Sound bites are the essential messages you want to convey. Talk out loud the most important ideas, concepts, and points of your topic as they relate to the idea you are pitching. Consider anecdotes, facts, statistics, stories, or something unlikely, unusual, controversial, shocking, funny, humorous, romantic, poignant, emotionally moving, or dramatic.

6. Make sure you're blurbable. By definition, a blurb is a very short advertisement or statement about a topic, product, or idea. For example, many book jackets have blurbs that are what people have said about the book.

The average sound bite on television is 10 seconds. Practice with a timer until you can speak your message in 10 to 20 seconds.

7. Get booked on local shows first. Even before you consider approaching "Oprah," get practice on your local news and talk shows. This will give you a chance to fine-tune your sound bites so you won't be shocked by the speed of national television. When you're a guest on the show you'll typically have a total of one to seven minutes to communicate your entire message—in 10- to 20-second increments. Once you have a good feel for the rhythm of television, you'll feel more relaxed and ready.

8. Wow the producers with brevity. The moment you open your mouth you are auditioning. Keep your list of talking points by the phone when you call a producer (or a

## A Good Pitch Page

- The four Ws
- Short bio of author or product founder
- Media experience of author or product founder
- Short description of what's unique
- How the show's audience is impacted by book or product
- A few sample interview questions
- More than one story angle
- Contact information

producer calls you) so you'll be succinct. Rehearse them so that they sound natural and inviting. Make sure all your points are targeted exactly to the angle you're proposing—making you (and your product) irresistible on the air.[1]

▪ ▪ ▪

Whether your public relations strategy lands you on "Oprah" or on the front page of a local newspaper, media attention is one of the most valuable tools you have when targeting the mom market. It increases your credibility, creates a buzz around your product, and reinforces your branding. The value of positive press far outweighs the investment you could make purchasing the same space of advertising in the same publication.

It takes creativity, timeliness, and unique story angles to obtain the attention of the media. To capture the business of the mom market through the media, you must present stories that represent the individuals of your target market, speak to the solutions they seek as mothers, and present a topic that is relevant to their concerns and desires. A strong public relations initiative can create an important tool from which to generate the most value marketing tool available to you: word of mom.

## CHAPTER ELEVEN

# Moms As Employees and Business Owners

M OMS ARE NOT only big business, they are big into business. It would be an injustice to the topic of marketing to mothers to omit a discussion of the mom market in the world of business. Few consumer-product companies or service providers take full advantage of the buying power of the mom market because they fail to recognize a mother in her role as an employee or business owner. Even the most successful marketers will stop short of tapping into the other wallet many mothers manage, that of her employer or, increasingly, the checkbook of her own company. After the lunchboxes are packed, the groceries bought, and the car fueled, moms are buying computers, leasing copiers, ordering books, and requesting shipments of supplies from all over the world.

In their roles as managers, contractors, service providers, manufacturers, and business owners, moms are driving a large part of the American economy. A lot of money is on the table for companies who include marketing to moms as employees or business owners. Companies have three basic opportunities for marketing to moms in business:

(1) as employers looking for valuable employees, (2) as vendors targeting female employees as decision makers, and (3) as vendors targeting business owners. In this chapter, we will take a look at the opportunities of each segment and how companies are capitalizing on serving them.

## Twenty Leading Occupations of Employed Women*

Managers and administrators
Secretaries
Cashiers
Registered nurses
Sales supervisors and proprietors
Elementary school teachers
Nursing aides, orderlies, and attendants
Bookkeepers and accounting and auditing clerks
Waitresses
Sales workers, retail and personal
Receptionists
Sales workers, other commodities
Accountants and auditors
Cooks
Investigators and adjusters, excluding insurance
Janitors and cleaners
Secondary school teachers
Hairdressers and cosmetologists
General office clerks
Administrative support occupations

*In order of number occupying position.

*Source:* U.S. Department of Labor, Bureau of Labor Statistics, "Annual Averages 2000," (Unpublished data: www.dol.gov).

Each day over 25 million mothers work outside of their duties as mother, wife, or homemaker.[1] Mothers are taking on roles as teachers, sales professionals, office administrators, doctors, lawyers, and truck drivers. Mothers go to work in governor's mansions, penthouse CEO offices, the Senate floor, and television studios. We have even seen working mothers in space. The jobs they assume are as varied as their hours and locations.

# The Importance of Attracting Mothers As Employees

IN ORDER TO fully integrate and execute a marketing plan to mothers, a company must position itself as an employer that attracts and retains mothers. The effort is important for many reasons. First, mothers expect companies to walk the talk. Moms will recognize inconsistencies in your marketing message if you are telling them in print that you are a company who serves mothers yet you do not serve them as employees. You also put yourself at risk that one day the media will reveal that only 20 percent of your workforce is women although you tout being a company who believes in women. It's easy to see the damage that can be done. Think back to what Kathie Lee Gifford experienced when the media began releasing reports that she was using child labor and under-paid women to manufacturer her apparel.

## CASE STUDY: AVON

Avon Products was named the top Fortune 1000 company for female executives by the National Association of Female Executives on its annual list in 2001.[2] Not only does Avon have a female chairwoman and CEO in Andrea Jung, but also, according to company information, Avon has more women in management positions (86 percent) than any other Fortune 500 company. Half of its board of directors are female. Avon has built itself on the strength of a female sales force, many of whom are mothers looking for a way to supplement their household income. Avon sends a clear message to mothers that it cares about women as individuals by supporting causes (such as breast cancer research) and valuing them as employees. The payoff could be seen in sales following the events of September 11, when most companies were experiencing the effects of a slipping economy. Avon, on the other hand, was able to leverage the personal relationships that its female workforce has with their customers and rely on the loyalty women have to the brand to avoid the deep sales losses that many other companies experienced.

## CASE STUDY: JOHNSON & JOHNSON

Johnson & Johnson has also successfully integrated its brand messages into the corporate culture. The company was named to the top slot of *Working Mother* magazine's 2001 list of "100 Best Companies for Working Mothers." The Johnson & Johnson credo outlines the corporation's responsibilities to the interests of its customers, employees, and the communities in which they live and work. Johnson & Johnson fulfills that promise through programs like the Women's Museum in Dallas, Texas, and by offering working parents benefits that allow them to balance their work and family needs. In addition, it supports innovative programs that serve the needs of female employees, such as Nurture Space (a program that features quiet, comfortable facilities and trained professional counselors to help new mothers succeed at breastfeeding while returning to work), flexible work schedules, on-site day care centers, and family absence policies.

Recently, Johnson & Johnson pledged $20 million for a drive to recruit nurses, a shrinking profession. Television commercials as well as scholarship programs will support the "Campaign for Nursing's Future." This strategy works because, as we have already learned, mothers want to know that the companies they are supporting are also supporting their families. In fact, according to a 1999 report released by the National Foundation for Women Business Owners (NFWBO), one in five working women agree that the social responsibility of companies is a major influence in their buying decisions.[3]

## RETAINING YOUR WORKING MOTHERS

According to U.S. Department of Labor estimates, the base cost of replacing a worker is 30 percent of that person's annual earnings.[4] Many mothers leave the workplace because of the inability to find suitable day care, as well as a disproportionate relationship between pay and work-related expenses, including those related to managing the demands of children. By offering flexible work schedules, day-care solutions, or other work-and-family-balance benefits, you will be able to reduce your turnover rate and save the costs associated with replacing employees. NationsBank (now Bank of America) found that offering a $25 per week childcare subsidy brought turnover among users down from 46 percent to 14 percent.[5]

Liz Claiborne, which tops *Working Mother* magazine's list of "Top 25 Companies for Executive Women," takes recruiting and retaining female employees very seriously. They see the value in retaining females and use technology to help them deliver flexibility to their working parents. In some situations this means allowing mothers to telecommute from home or teleconference into meetings.

"The days of companies being considered progressive for allowing flexible schedules, telecommuting, or job sharing are virtually over. It is a competitive disadvantage if you do not acknowledge the needs of today's diverse workforce," says Larry McClure, senior vice president of Human Resources for Liz Claiborne. "Mothers are one critical segment of this constituency. It takes creativity and, in some cases, courage to challenge the norm and shape policies and practices that allow these smart, insightful employees to make valuable contributions at work while tending to their lives at home. Technology has enabled us to more easily balance these two competing forces."

You don't have to earn a spot on top of *Working Mother's* list to successfully market yourself to mothers. Your company will be able to retain mothers as employees by providing work and family benefits that offer them solutions. In order to determine what benefits matter most to working mothers, view them as you would a customer. Research your market, determine the need, offer a product, and market it. Begin by asking your employees what they want and need. Is it flexible work hours or concierge services that motivate your working mothers? Is it job sharing or childcare reimbursement? Not only will your employees appreciate your interest in their opinions but also you are likely to identify employment needs that are unique to your business. Some could be quite inexpensive to implement.

For example, I know of one company where the working mothers' only request was a couch in the restroom so that they could sit and use a breast pump comfortably. The request was met the same day by moving a sofa from a departed executive's office into the ladies lounge. The result was renewed employee morale, which translated into increased productivity.

We polled working mothers on BlueSuitMom.com as to the work/life benefit they valued the most. Over half of the 794 respondents said flexible work hours; 35 percent said on-site childcare. Recent studies show that employers are beginning to recognize that many of their employees would like flexibility in

## Work/Life Benefits Popular with Blue-Suit Mothers

| | |
|---|---|
| Flexible hours | On-site health clubs |
| On-site childcare | Tuition reimbursement |
| Childcare subsidy | Elder care programs |
| Personal leave | College savings plans |
| Counseling services | Adoption assistance |
| Casual dress | Fitness club benefits |
| Employee entertain- | Additional family and |
| ment/company | medical leave |
| product discounts | Dry-cleaning service |
| Telecommuting | Catered meals |
| Concierge services | |

*Source:* BlueSuitMom.com, 2002.

choosing the hours they work.[6] In 1997, more than 25 million workers (27.6 percent of all full-time workers) varied their work hours to some degree. The percentage of workers taking advantage of flexible hours has more than doubled since 1985, the first year the Bureau of Labor Statistic started collecting the data.[7] Telecommuting is also becoming a popular benefit with more than 6.5 million Americans (not including the self-employed) telecommuting during the week.

As an employer you want to attract the most valuable employees to your company. As the number of working mothers continues to grow, more of those future employees will be mothers. To remain competitive, offer attractive compensation packages with benefits that mothers value. A study by the Radcliffe Public Policy Center found that 61 percent of Americans would be willing to take a pay cut if it meant more time with their children or other family members.[8]

Benefits are becoming increasingly valuable to all employees. September 11 has impacted nearly every aspect of American living, including the way we view our employment. As Americans are reprioritizing their lives, finding ways to balance work and family is becoming more important.

## CASE STUDY: SURE FIT'S FLEXIBLE SCHEDULES AND TELECOMMUTING

Sure Fit recognized the importance of offering mothers flexible work schedules as a means to getting the best talent possible for their business. In their effort to offer mothers a solution for balancing work and family, they acquire more effective employees.

"At Sure Fit, many of our employees work from home. We started the at-home program about three years ago," says

Lynn Monek, director of Sure Fit's customer service division. "By allowing our representatives to work from home we have been able to retain excellent customer service reps who would have left our employment due to pregnancy or childcare issues. By utilizing at-home staff we have freed up seats in the call center and were able to hire more people in house."

Lori Schlemmer started as an administrative assistant in customer service. When her first child was born, Sure Fit created a position for her to work from home. She now works for up to 30 hours a week from her home office.

"When the offer to work from home was presented to me, it seemed like the perfect solution to balancing my work schedule and my new role as a mom," says Schlemmer, who answers e-mail inquiries from Sure Fit's Web site. "The hours I work are completely flexible. I try to keep a schedule of the days that I work, such as Monday, Tuesday, Thursday, and one day on the weekend, but my hours are not always the same. The work is available to me 24 hours a day. I am more productive at home because I do not have the distractions that can sometimes occur in a large office. The benefits of working at home are tremendous—I can spend more time with my children. The commute to the office can take up to an hour one-way, so I save up to 2 hours a day by working from home. I can work more hours because the work is always available to me. I also save money on automobile expenses such as gas and maintenance and I don't have to pay for child care."

At Sure Fit, the work-at-home policy started with Liana Toscanini. "I began as a full-time employee working in the New York office," she explains. "In my case, I thought I had a marketable skill that was easily transferable to a home office environment. It's all writing, faxes, e-mails, and calls."

When Toscanini moved to Massachusetts, Sure Fit didn't want to lose such a valuable employee. The company president hired Toscanini as vice president of Insurgence. "Insurgence means challenging authority," says Toscanini. "I am more of a creative type, a guerilla marketer—I end up challenging the corporate view a lot. My responsibilities include Web, catalog (direct marketing), and public relations."

Toscanini travels to New York once a week for face-to-face meetings. The rest of the week she works at home. "I take breaks during the day to get some exercise or do errands or have meetings for my volunteer work," she says. "On average, I work about eight to ten hours a day for Sure Fit. It works out well. By working at home I get more work done. Writing requires quiet and no interruptions. I also find that I am in better health because there is less stress and I have the ability to fit exercise in."

The majority of Sure Fit's work-at-home employees are in its customer service division. To work from home all one needs is a phone and a computer. Sure Fit currently has twenty customer service agents working from home, five of them full-time and the rest part-time. By allowing the reps to work from home, Sure Fit has been able to retain excellent customer service reps who would otherwise have left the company due to childcare issues. Many of them have small children and want to be at home with them.

## SIGNS OF PROGRESS IN THE CORPORATE WORLD

The efforts made by companies to market themselves to mothers as employees have grown. According to Patrick

McCarthy, associate professor of Industrial and Organizational Psychology, Middle Tennessee State University, the trend has increased because companies have now the felt the benefits of these programs. Says McCarthy, "With such traditional icons of business as *Fortune* and *Business Week* giving featured attention repeatedly to the business benefits of being family-friendly, it seems the scope of such progress is likely to continue expanding. Businesses used to view work-family initiatives as 'nice little HR perks.'"

But according to McCarthy, those companies also often viewed such initiatives as a cost and inconvenience. Somewhere along the way, a more progressive conceptualization began to emerge. They shifted from a cost view to an investment view—an investment with a payoff of significant, tangible business benefits. When impressive quantifiable evidence of those benefits emerged, then businesses could see the value of work-family initiatives in their own bottom-line language. "More companies are beginning to realize these initiatives aren't just nice things to do for employees," says McCarthy, "they have substantial benefits to the organizations as well."

# Approaching Moms As Decision Makers

WORKING MOTHERS ARE spending billions of their employer's dollars. In 1999, *Working Mother* magazine reported that there were over 15 million career-committed mothers and that almost half held managerial or above positions within their corporations.[9] In addition, the market is growing in size and influence. According to Catalyst, the nonprofit research and advisory organization working to advance women in business and the professions, the number of female corporate officers in Fortune 500 companies has risen from 8.7 percent to 12.5 percent in the past six years.[10] Promotions of women such as Betsy Holden (to president and chief executive of Kraft Foods North America) and Meg Whitman (to CEO of eBay) illustrate the new level of professional success working mothers are achieving within corporate America.

Executive working mothers are making buying decisions on behalf of their companies at all levels. Within my own network of mothers, one manages a multimillion-dollar budget for Motorola as director of operations and another a million-dollar budget for a top university.

The marketing approach necessary to capture this market is created in your corporate culture. Today's businesswomen are smart, savvy, and knowledgeable about female-friendly businesses. Over four million people visited *Working Mother* magazine's Web site in October when they released their "Top 100 Best Companies for Working Mothers" annual list. Subtle messages can tell women that you recognize their place in business. For instance, Office Depot does a good job of this in their latest ads with Kathy Ireland.

## CASE STUDY: OFFICE DEPOT

In one of Office Depot's recent ads, two businesswomen are walking to the office commenting on whether or not a lady can wear white shoes after Labor Day. They are approached by Kathy Ireland, who sets them straight on their etiquette debate. The ad then proceeds to tell viewers that when it comes to answers in the office, you can turn to Office Depot for help. In a subtle way it lets the audience know that Office

Depot recognizes the place of women in making buying decisions in the workplace.

The positioning you establish in developing your image
as a mom-friendly employer will go a long way in differenti-
ating your company from your competitors. Although pricing will always play a part in who gets the contract, your
corporate reputation can be the deciding factor in earning
the business. It's part of the association factor of doing business with businesses that mirror your own beliefs. No one
wants to associate their business with another business that
can damage their reputation.

## It's in the Details

Women notice the small things when it comes to vendor relations. It is part of the difference in how men and women
view relationships in general. I mention this because, as a
vendor, it is important to take into account the details of
your relationship without pandering to gender difference.
My point is best illustrated by a common mistake vendors
often make when it comes to leave-behinds.

While in the newspaper business I once received roses
from a vendor trying to get his foot in the door. It was a gesture that he obviously would not have made if I had been
male. The gesture was totally inappropriate and demonstrated his lack of respect for me as a businesswoman. A
more appropriate leave-behind would have been a dual-gen-
der gift, such as an office clock, nice pen, or duffel bag.

As another example, a vendor distributed logo-imprinted
watches to the executives of an auto company. The watches
were all male watches. Clearly this vendor did not appreciate
the decision-making power of the female executives.

Marketing yourself to businesswomen should be an integrated approach, involving how you brand your company in the eyes of all moms, whether they are retail consumers, employees, or business clients.

# The Vital Statistics on Women-Owned Businesses*

THE FOLLOWING NUMBERS speak for themselves:

■ There are an estimated 6.2 million majority-owned, privately held women-owned firms in the United States, accounting for 28 percent of all privately held firms in the country.

■ Women-owned firms in the United States employ 9.2 million people and generate $1.15 trillion in sales.

■ In the last five years, the number of women-owned firms increased by 14 percent nationwide, twice the rate of the average of all firms (7 percent).

■ There are 112,712 women-owned firms with revenues of $1 million or more and 8,480 with 100 or more employees in the United States.

■ While the largest share of women-owned firms (53 percent) is in the service sector, women are diversifying into nontraditional industries including construction and agriculture.

Statistics courtesy of the Center for Women's Business Research, (Washington, D.C.: Key Facts, 2001).

# Moms As Business Owners

THE MARKET OF moms as business owners is a great and untapped niche. Few people fully appreciate the magnitude of female-owned businesses in the United States. The "Vital Statistics" sidebar demonstrates the growing magnitude and diversity of women-owned businesses.

A large majority of these women are mothers. And if you reach these mothers, they will buy your product at home as well as in the office. A study by the Center for Women's Business Research revealed that 86 percent of women entrepreneurs say they use the same products and services at home that they do in their business, for familiarity and convenience.[11]

Women are starting their businesses in offices, factories, and at home. The latter is one of the fastest growing segments of women-owned businesses. Many are mothers seeking a way to increase their professional fulfillment as well as find a solution to balancing work and family. Although many of these businesses were started out of well-conceived planning, others, such as SoapWorks and Baby Einstein videos, were created out of the experience of being a mom.

## REACHING MOMPRENUERS

Service providers and companies who recognize mompreneurs through advertising and marketing have the potential to capture revenue being ignored by others. So how do you reach this mom-owned business market? With even a limited marketing budget you can communicate your message to these mothers through banners, sponsorships, and electronic newsletter ads. For those with a large budget,

Office Depot's strategy, which is discussed below, is worth exploring.

### A Closely Networked Group

Fortunately the momprenuer segment is a closely networked group of women. The Internet joins a large number of them together on places where they compare notes, get advice, and pool resources. It is easy to find these moms on sites such as Home-Based Working Mothers, www.hbwm.com, LittleDidIKnow.com, www.LDIK.com, and Work at Home Moms, www.wahm.com.

When positioning your company with momprenuers, focus on offering solutions for running their business more efficiently. Recognize the unique challenges of these mothers in keeping their business separate from their family, especially when both are located in the home.

## CASE STUDY: OFFICE DEPOT HITS THE BULL'S-EYE

Office Depot has made a clear decision to target women-owned businesses, recognizing that many are also mothers. Aside from creating ads that feature females, they are sponsoring special events designed for female business owners, sponsoring family causes, and positioning ads in local female business publications (as well as parenting magazines during back-to-school season).

Office Depot ran an ad recently that hit the bull's-eye with home-based working women. The ad pictured a woman in her home office with this copy: "It's not a corner office with a view of the city. But it's where you do your best work. That's why your home office has to be special. From office furnishings to the latest technology, Office Depot is the expert source to provide you with what you need when you need it." The ad speaks straight to the pride a woman takes in her surroundings, her talents as a professional, and the convenience women appreciate and need.

### Sponsoring Networking

Sponsoring a networking event is an inexpensive way to reach all mom business owners, regardless of where their office is located. Women business owners like to compare ideas and they like to be recognized as *real* businesses. Hosting some type of mixer or educational program accomplishes both of these objectives.

A bank, for instance, might host an after-hour happy hour with a short program entitled, "Obtaining small business loans for expanding your company," letting the audience know that the bank recognizes the potential of women-owned businesses. If special event planning is not your forte, contact a local chapter of the National Association of Women Business Owners (NAWBO) or National Association of Female Executives (NAFE) and sponsor a meeting.

In addition, consider print advertising in local niche publications, such as business dailies or parenting newspapers. A few years ago, I applauded a local bank for its creativity when it ran ads in *South Florida Parenting* magazine, which targeted mothers as potential employees. The ads highlighted the benefits that a career as a part-time teller presented to mothers. It was a creative way to speak with a meaningful message to their target audience.

If your budget is more in line with that of Office Depot, you may want to consider looking at the many opportunities that *Working Mother* magazine offers beyond traditional print advertising. The parent company of the magazine, Working Mother Media, offers event sponsorships and custom publications, as well as many other ways to touch the working mom market. At the risk of being self-promoting, my own company, BSM Media, offers original programs designed to help clients reach the niche of mothers. In addition to custom newsletters and content, we produce Web sites, radio pro-

## A Word of Warning Regarding Diversity Marketing

THERE IS A BIG difference between marketing to working mothers and marketing to diversity issues. To find examples of companies presenting off-target ads all you have to do is flip through a recent copy of Working Mother magazine. A full-page MasterCard ad said, "Our employees are not all cut from the same cloth, but together they make up our fabric." I'm sure the objective of the ad was to communicate to working mothers that MasterCard values all types of employees, regardless of ethnic background or gender. This message is important to working mothers but doesn't speak to them in meaningful language. That is, this ad doesn't address the needs or interests of working mothers. As a marketing professional, I see it as a generic diversity ad that MasterCard probably uses in any one of many ethnic publications. Remember the lessons of chapter 4? Moms want to be able to see themselves in your ad.

gramming, and campaigns targeted at momprenuers. (You can learn more by visiting www.marketingtomoms.com.)

If your company is going to spend the money to place advertising in a niche publication, make certain you speak to the market in relevant language. Marketing budgets should never be wasted.

For an ad that hits its mark, look at the Lilly's ad in a recent issue of *Working Mother*. This ad pictures the partial face of a woman, focusing on her eyes, and says, "Your priorities look like ours. I want challenge in my work, time with my family to make a difference. Lilly seeks answers to the world's most pressing unmet medical needs. We are also committed to proactively addressing the needs of our employees. For the past seven years, *Working Mother* has recognized that we are serious about work-life balance."

Vivendi Universal also does a good job at recognizing the needs and lifestyle of working mothers in their ad titled, "Let your family grow with ours." The message is, "At Vivendi Universal, we understand that life can be challenging with the constant demands of balancing schedules, career advancement, keeping up with the information age and caring for your family. That's why we offer personalized support programs, like on-site and back-up childcare, flexible work arrangements, scholarship programs, paid maternity/paternity/adoption leave and on-site New Mother's Rooms. Working together with our employees and families to achieve their goals is a challenge we address every day— because what's most important in our life is your life."

■　■　■

Incorporating a marketing plan to connect with mothers as employees and business owners can present many opportunities. Not only will it help you tap into the billions of dollars being spent by working mothers from their offices but also it will help you retain the best employees, increase productivity, boost employee morale, strengthen your consumer image, and create avenues for expansion. It only takes recognizing the potential of the market, finding the right message, and integrating it throughout your entire company.

## CHAPTER TWELVE

# The Results of Our Research: Talking to Real Moms

W E'VE HEARD FROM marketing executives. Now it's time to hear from the moms. We went directly to the source of this trillion-dollar market and asked moms for their thoughts on advertising and marketing and what elements of each drive their buying decisions. I enlisted the help of Prange & O'Hearn's Insights, Inc., a research and marketing services firm based in Stuart, Florida. The firms that Prange & O'Hearn have worked with include Pro Player Stadium, JM Family Enterprises/Southeast Toyota, AT&T Wireless Services, SC Johnson Wax, and the Florida Marlins.

Prange & O'Hearn and BSM Media designed a questionnaire to use in our study. The purpose of the study was to quantify the opinions and attitudes of moms regarding advertising for products and services targeted to mothers and its impact on them as consumers.

# Survey Methodology

THE DATABASE OF e-mail addresses was comprised of customer information from BlueSuitMom.com, BabyUniverse .com, LittleDidIKnow.com, and other sites that are known to have content of interest to mothers. Respondents received an e-mail message requesting their participation in the survey through electronic newsletters and independent e-mails.

Those who agreed to participate clicked a link to Insights, Inc.'s Web site, which connected them directly to the questionnaire. Questionnaire responses were entered by clicking check boxes, selecting predefined choices from pull-down menus, and entering open-end responses. Questionnaires were filled out by 461 mothers from all over the United States. (In addition, we personally interviewed an additional fifty mothers in depth.)

As each survey was completed, it was captured in Insights, Inc.'s database for tabulation. A cookie was used to control the possibility of multiple responses from the same computer. The information we received was not only interesting but valuable. (Additional survey results and information can be found at www.marketingtomoms.com.)

In addition to presenting the quantitative results of the questionnaire, I have included the comments of real-life moms so that you have the benefit of being part of the word-of-mom network. I think you'll find what they have to say interesting.

# Demographics

OVER 86 PERCENT of our respondents were twenty-five to forty-four years old, with 9 percent representing a group over forty-five, and only 5 percent made up of those under twenty-five. Over 76 percent have incomes of at least $50,000 or higher, higher than the average U.S. household income.

When it comes to the number of children, 45 percent have one child, 36 percent have two children, and only 15 percent have three or more. Eighty percent of our respondents have at least one child under the age of six. Ninety percent of our mothers are married.

Mothers are busy people. Only 20 percent of our moms are not employed at all. The remaining 80 percent are employed either part- or full-time, some in offices and others in home businesses. Fifty percent are employed full-time outside the home. On average they work 30 hours a week and report to spending an additional 6.5 hours a week at home working on employment-related responsibilities. Over 60 percent describe their job as a professional, managerial, or support position.

When they are not working or taking care of their families, our moms are using media for entertainment and information. They average 2.08 hours a day watching television and just as much time listening to the radio. Newspapers get less of mom's attention than either radio or television on a daily basis.

Over a week's time, moms said they spend just 3.33 hours reading a local newspaper. National newspapers such as the *Wall Street Journal, USA Today,* or the *New York Times* get even less of a mother's time than local papers. Moms said they read or look through a national newspaper less than once a week. Magazines, on the other hand, get a piece of our mother's busy schedule. Our respondents said that they read or leaf through more than four magazines per month.

# Marketing Opportunities: Mom's Answers

OUR RESEARCH CONFIRMS that mothers manage a large amount of household revenue. In just our small group of mothers, the household income totals over $100 million. The opportunities to tap into these and other mom-controlled wallets lie in four results revealed in our research. First, only 20 percent of mothers think print advertising is doing either extremely well or well in speaking to mothers. This leaves 80 percent of the mom market that thinks print advertising is only doing an okay to not-good-at-all job in speaking to moms. Second, only 25 percent of mothers think television advertising is doing a good job connecting with the mom market. This means that over 70 percent think television advertisers are doing an okay to not-good-at-all job in speaking to mothers. Third, only 38 percent of mothers feel that companies recognize and acknowledge the needs of mothers in their advertising campaigns.

Finally, we asked moms, "How often do you see an advertisement that, in your opinion, sends the wrong message to moms?" Over 50 percent of respondents said they see ads often or very often that send the wrong message to moms. Here lies the opportunity. Marketers who speak to moms with a message that is relevant, valuable, and in a language they understand will capture the buying power of mothers. As we review our results, you will see other opportunities emerge. You will also see that there are many more well-defined behaviors and opinions in the mom market. These insights will help you in establishing a meaningful relationship with mothers.

# Word of Mom

WE ASKED MOTHERS how they made first-time buying decisions when purchasing products for home, children, and self. In all three categories, mothers said overwhelmingly that they are very likely to purchase a product that a friend or relative recommends to them. When contemplating purchases for home and self, over 55 percent of mothers rely on recommendations and the number jumps to 64 percent if the product is for their children. Child-product companies especially should leverage the networking abilities of mothers to gain full potential of the market.

**Q.** *Why do mothers value the opinions of other mothers for product recommendations and suggestions?*

**A.** "I usually ask other mothers who have experienced using the product. I figure that they know what works best because they have used it with their own children. Most moms tend to have their own favorite products, and what I notice is that they not only recommend products to other mothers, but if they have to purchase a gift for another mother, they will often give those products they endorse."

DEBBI, MOTHER OF TWO, AGES 16 MONTHS AND 4 MONTHS.

**A.** "I think it is the matter of trust that moms talk to other moms. It's foolproof. You aren't going believe a commercial for a product over someone who has actually used the product. It is timesaving when you can use the opinion of another because you don't have to spend the time researching. The fact that it worked for someone else is enough for me. I tend to use the advice of others more with household items rather than for children's products. Kids tend to have more of their own opinions so even if another mother likes it, your child's decision will determine if you buy it."

LISA, MOTHER OF FOUR, AGES 19, 16, 14, 8.

**A.** "I listen to mothers because they have tried the product. Another mom would not recommend it if she had not gotten good results while using it herself."

SUSAN, MOTHER OF ONE, AGE 9.

**A.** "I think moms talk to other moms because they just want to make sure the decision they make is correct. They know what they want to do or buy but hearing it from someone else just makes them feel better about doing it. We love when people agree with us. It validates what we already know as mothers."

CHRIS, MOTHER OF TWO, AGES 11 AND 8.

# Loyalty of Moms

WE ASKED MOMS about the likelihood that they would purchase a product for their home, child, or self based on their past experience with it. Ninety percent of moms said they were very likely to purchase a product for their home based on prior experience. In the child and self categories, the responses were 85 percent and 82 percent, respectively. Performance plays an important role in a mother's decision to buy a product. Mothers are looking for timesaving solutions and convenience. Moms will stay loyal to those products that eliminate their need to spend time searching for a new product. It is clear that if a company wins the admiration of a mother, she will continue to buy their product.

Q. *If you are happy with a product you buy for your family, are you more likely to keep buying it and why?*

A. "Certainly I will continue to buy any product with which I am happy if it meets three simple criteria. First, it must be liked, used, or enjoyed by my family. Second, it must perform consistently, and last, it must be within a relative cost margin to its competitive equal. It's okay for it to cost a little more, but not too much. My personal tolerance seems to be about 10 percent if it's a family favorite."

FAB, MOTHER OF THREE, AGES 14, 13, AND 10.

A. "When I buy a product that I am happy with, I am more likely to keep buying it. The trick is finding products that demonstrate consistent quality. We are committed to products that are natural and nontoxic. When I buy items that match these standards, I continue using them."

RONI, MOTHER OF TWO, AGES 27 AND 23.

A. "I have a busy life, so when I find a product that works for my children I will keep buying it because it saves me time and the effort of searching for something else. It has already proven its benefit for my family."

TRACY, MOTHER OF TWO, AGES 8 AND 5.

# In the Park, at Work, or on the Phone: Where Moms Talk

WE KNOW THAT moms are talking to other moms about products and services. In order to find out where moms are talking to each other, we asked moms how often they are in various places when discussing products or services. It is not surprising that 52 percent said that it was often to very often that they spoke to other moms on the telephone at home. It seems that a lot of conversations are happening in the office as well. Forty-one percent of mothers said they often to very often speak with other moms at their place of employment about buying products. However, slightly more mothers are conversing with other mothers about products through e-mail than are talking around the water cooler. Forty-two percent of mothers said they talk to other mothers through e-mail about products for their children.

**Q.** *Where are you most often when you are talking to other mothers about products or services for your family?*

**A.** "Women tend to have a lot of girlfriends who they talk to, gather and share information with at the soccer field or at school. Moms are great communicators about products that work for their families. Most of my women friends are the ones who not only buy our own clothes but also are the designated shopper for the kid's school clothes, shoes, and even the groceries. . . . Moms compare notes on all these things while watching sports with other moms or in line at their child's school."

NANCY, MOTHER OF TWO, AGES 17 AND 12.

**A.** "When the children were younger I would talk to moms at the park about different products but now that they are older, I tend to have those conversations at the ball field during games."

EMILY, MOTHER OF THREE, AGES 9, 7, AND 4.

**A.** "I tend to have conversations with other mothers at events our children are involved in, like while waiting for dance class to conclude or at a baseball practice."

MELODI, MOTHER OF THREE, AGES 10, 9, AND 5.

# Moms Online

IT IS CLEAR that moms rely on the recommendations of other moms when it comes to product information. In fact, information in general is a valuable commodity for mothers. Seventy-eight percent of mothers said they are more likely to buy from a company that provides useful parenting or health information than one that does not. Where do moms go to find this information outside of their friends and family?

We asked our mothers, "When you are seeking information about products and services for your child, how likely are you to use the Internet, newspapers, magazines, or direct mail materials?" According to our results, moms head to the Internet. Seventy-one percent said they were very likely to use the Internet for information. It far exceeds the use of any other channel. In fact, this is the only instance where friends and families do not serve as the number one source of information. It appears that moms will collect information online and then turn to other moms for validation before purchasing products for their children.

Mothers indicated that they also turn to their doctor or pediatrician for advice and, again, magazines appeared on the list of likely sources for information.

**Q.** *How do you use the Internet for information?*

**A.** "I always back up my choices with reading *Consumer Reports* and generally also check on the Internet for update "recall" information on baby products especially, which can also make me crazy! I never really shopped online until I had my first child, and now I look there first, before spending time loading children and car seats into cars to shop—what a trip! Also, I work and spend many hours on the phone and in meetings. So I need to know that my shopping hours are strategically well spent."

MICHELLE, MOTHER OF TWO, AGES 3 YEARS AND 8 MONTHS.

**A.** "I will use the Internet to research items that I intend to buy that cost over $50. I always go to Consumer Reports online to research a product if it is over $50. They have a good site with ratings for durability and safety information. I recently bought a new phone. I researched the product on Consumer Reports but then a search engine took me to eBay. They also provided a lot of information on the phone and I ultimately bought it new on eBay after reading their product information. I read *Consumer Reports* magazine for product reviews but when there is a specific purchase I need to make, I will go online to find facts on that item. It's convenient and easy."

JILL, MOTHER OF TWO, AGES 8 AND 5.

**A.** "I use the Internet for homework and correspondence with other women. I converse with the other mothers through e-mail because it is convenient and I can do it on my own time. I also know that if I send an e-mail I'm not intruding on someone else's time. If you call a mom, you have no idea what they are busy doing, but with e-mail, they can talk with you at their convenience. The Internet has taken the place of the nightly trip to the library when doing our children's homework. Now we just go to the den and type in our subject. We use Yahoo!, AskJeeves, and Google to find answers. AskJeeves is the most user friendly because you just type in a word or two and the answer comes right up. It makes homework help easy."

JANET, MOTHER OF THREE, AGES 13, 12, AND 11.

A. "I am a real research person when it comes to buying a product. When I recently renovated my house, I went online to product manufacturer sites such as KitchenAid to find information on the product before I bought it. I also used Consumer Reports online and off to give me unbiased opinions."

DIANE, MOTHER OF TWO, AGES 8 AND 5.

A. "I use the Internet to gather information about family travel destinations, for shopping, and to help my children with homework projects. I normally go the Internet before I make a purchase so I may research the product and make a wise buying decision. I even went online to research tiki bars when my husband and I were thinking of adding one to our backyard."

ELLEN, MOTHER OF THREE, AGES 10, 7, AND 6.

A. "I go online anytime I need to research anything, whether it is to make vacation plans or to find activities for my children. During the holidays, I tend to do a lot of shopping online."

MARY PAT, MOTHER OF FIVE, AGES 17, 15, 12, 10, AND 4.

# Shopping Online

MOTHERS ARE EVENLY divided on how they find Web sites. Mothers said they equally use search engines and URLs they see in print publications to find Web sites for information or to make purchases. Included in print publications were magazines, newspapers, and direct mail pieces. Slightly fewer mothers said they go to sites at the recommendation of friends and relatives. Television advertising serves as the least effective means of driving traffic to Web sites. In fact, more mothers find a Web site by surfing the Internet than they do through television.

Moms are spending money on the Internet. Only 6 percent of mothers said they have never made a purchase using the Internet. The Web is also serving as a persuasive marketing tool. Over 60 percent of mothers said they are somewhat likely to purchase a product for their home or child from something they see or read on the Internet; 57 percent are somewhat likely to purchase a product for themselves. Among their favorite sites, mothers list Babycenter.com and iVillage.com.

**Q.** *What products do you purchase for yourself and your family online? Where do you spend your money online?*

**A.** "I buy all of my children's summer reading books online. I love Amazon for all the latest CDs and DVDs. Amazon makes it easy to purchase online because they will suggest products by the age of my children. This makes it easy for me because then I don't have to know the difference between Britney Spears and Metallica. If I'm online buying a book, I may pick up a suggested item, too. It saves me the time of figuring it out where the shop I need is in the mall. I do groceries online especially for the staples that our family goes through every week. This makes my life easy because I don't have to run out every time I need cat food or dog food."

JORJ, MOTHER OF THREE, AGES 24, 18, AND 14.

A. "I do a lot of shopping on the Internet. I've bought Legos on eToys and phonics materials on eBay but it is not only things for the kids that I purchase online. I buy clothes at Nordstrom.com. I think that is the best Web site out there. They have made it so easy. All I need is a catalog number and item numbers and the shopping is done. I don't have to dig through pages of merchandise. It makes it convenient and easy to buy items I need."

MARY, MOTHER OF TWO, AGE 7 (TWINS).

A. "Usually I shop online at the same places that I would shop if I made the trip to a store. There are some instances, though, that I shop at sites like HannahAnderson.com because we don't have a retail location close by. I buy my work clothes online at AnnTaylor.com or sometimes at BlueFly.com because they have a lot of good bargains. The Internet saves me the time it would take to go to the mall, and really I don't have the inclination to drag my children through the mall when my time is limited with them already. I buy a lot of kid's books and Pottery Barn items for my children online."

LAURA, MOTHER OF TWO, AGES 7 AND 5.

# What Moms Read

MAGAZINES HAVE APPEARED as an important medium in the mom market. We have already seen that the average mother reads or looks through 4.12 magazines a month. But mothers on average have 3.41 different magazines delivered to their home. Fifty-four percent of mothers said they were somewhat likely to use magazines when seeking product information for their child. What are the titles that moms feel are indispensable? We asked our moms if they could read or look through only two magazines a month, what would they read? The answers were numerous but the front-runners were *Parenting, Parents, People, Better Homes and Gardens,* and *Working Mother* magazines.

**Q.** *What are your attitudes on magazines?*

**A.** "I actually read more magazines than books. Magazines tend to be more available because I can pick one up in the check-out line at the grocery store. They are shorter and provide quick information. Right now, I am reading magazine articles on how to get my children to eat vegetables. The information I find in magazines can help me solve problems around my home and with my children. I read *Good Housekeeping, Family Circle,* and *Southern Living* for their recipes. I really like *Child* because they give you an age-specific child guide. It's a great way to know exactly what your child should be doing at each developmental stage."

MAUREEN, MOTHER OF THREE, AGES 8, 7, AND 3.

**A.** "I read *People* and *Sports Illustrated,* as well as others. I have to read *Sports Illustrated* to keep up with my family, who are very involved in athletics. I like *People* because it is just relaxing to read. I will often let my magazines stack up and then I take them on a trip with me when I'm not with my children which gives me time to read them."

JALIMA, MOTHER OF TWO, AGES 9 AND 7.

**A.** "Magazines are light and easy to pick up and read quickly. You can do more than one thing while you are reading a magazine."

ROBIN, MOTHER OF TWO, AGES 10 AND 8.

# Advertising to Moms

MOMS CONFIRMED THAT magazines are a good way to reach them with your marketing message. We asked, "What is the best way for a company to reach you with an advertising message?" Respondents had the opportunity to include their first and second best means of communication. Surprisingly, more mothers responded that magazines were better than television, radio, or e-mail. Forty-three percent of mothers said magazines were either the first or second best way to reach them with their advertising message. Television presented the next most successful way to reach a mother with mail following slightly behind. Telemarketers and moms don't mix. Telephone communication received less than 1 percent of the vote.

Two interesting trends emerged. First, newspapers only received 18 percent of moms' vote as a successful way to relay your marketing message. Second, moms expressed an appreciation for e-mail. Over eighty-five percent of mothers said they have interacted with retailers through e-mails.

**Q.** *If you could tell a company the best way to reach you with their advertising message, what would it be?*

**A.** "When it comes to buying product, I am more likely to purchase something that I've seen in a magazine article.

The fact that it is featured in an article tells me that a consumer has actually used it rather than a slick ad from a manufacturer trying to get me to buy the product. I read *Lucky* magazine because the experience is like vicarious shopping."

SUSAN, MOTHER OF ONE, AGE 9.

A. "Radio is the best way for an advertiser to reach me because I have it on 99 percent of the day, either in the house or in the car. I'm in the car so many hours of the day while driving my kids to school, sports, or other activities and the radio is always on. It's a good way to get the message to me."

NANCY, MOTHER OF TWO, AGES 8 AND 2.

A. "The best way to reach me is during "Friends" on Thursday nights. It is the only time during the week that I allow myself to watch television. I let the kids put themselves to bed and park myself in front of the television set for uninterrupted time."

ROBIN, MOTHER OF TWO, AGES 10 AND 8.

A. "The best way for marketers to reach me is through my children on children's TV channels. Because I am single, my children are more involved in the decision-making process of spending our household money. It is more convenient for me to have their help in our purchases. A single mom tends to spend a lot of time with her children so they are always there when I am shopping."

MONICA, MOTHER OF TWO, AGES 8 AND 7.

## Most Effective Ads

ONCE YOU HAVE a mother's attention, what ads are most effective in selling your product? The most effective ads, according to our mothers, are ones that focus on the benefits of the product. Over 50 percent said that ads focusing on product benefits were very effective in earning their business. In particular, moms appreciate ads that offer solutions for their busy lives.

**Q.** *What kinds of ads get your attention?*

**A.** "Ads that describe positive features of a product would get my attention at a glance. Because of my schedule, if I had to research the product (no matter how good it looks on paper), chances are I would quickly direct my focus to other areas."

BETTI, MOTHER OF THREE, AGES 18, 16, AND 14.

**A.** "I consider products that the family happens to benefit from. I buy these types of products on a repeated basis if they help give me some control over my day, help me complete a task efficiently, or make me believe I'm doing something good for my family."

BONNIE, MOTHER OF TWO, AGES 4 AND 2.

**A.** "I find ads that state the benefits of the product more effective because they offer you additional information that you may have had questions about. I also appreciate ads that explain specific uses, suggestions, or warnings about the product."

NANCY, MOTHER OF TWO, AGES 8 AND 2.

**A.** "I look for the benefit of quality because I don't have the time to re-shop for something that falls apart days after I buy it."

KIM, MOTHER OF TWO, AGES 8 AND 5.

**A.** "I am influenced by ads that show they relate to my stressful life. I like the ads that offer a way to squeeze an extra ten minutes into my busy life."

CECELIA, MOTHER OF TWO, AGES 8, 7, AND 3.

**A.** "I look for ads that represent well-known brands. The reputation of a product matters when it represents a brand known for safety. When it comes to my children, I want to know that a product is safe."

MIN, MOTHER OF TWO, AGES 9 AND 1.

# Setting the Picture

Mothers also ranked ads that feature children high on their list of effectiveness. Seventy-five percent said that such ads were very to somewhat effective. This type of ad seems to rely heavily on the mother's desire to see herself and her family in advertising.

**Q.** *How likely are you to buy a product if the ad features a child in it?*

**A.** "I am more likely to buy something . . . if there is a cute baby in it or if I can relate to seeing my child in it, especially if it is children's clothing. I think in general moms like to see ads that mimic their own lives."

PAM, MOTHER OF ONE, AGE 4.

**A.** "Ads that feature children are effective in that they strike a maternal chord in me. The pictures bring out my natural desire to protect, nurture, and enhance the lives of my own children."

BECKY, MOTHER OF TWO, AGES 12 AND 9.

$A.$ "I do believe ads which feature children are effective in marketing to mothers as we inherently believe in the honesty of children. . . . Even though on an intellectual level we know the ads are scripted, I believe there is more of a tendency to believe in the sincerity of a child than an adult in the same situation."

MINDY, MOTHER OF TWO, AGES 2½ YEARS AND 2½ MONTHS.

$A.$ "Ads with happy energetic children attract my attention because that's the image of what I want for my family. Moms frequently buy something to satisfy a desire to achieve happiness and peace. My children are attracted to ads and often call my attention to those which interest them."

NATALIE, MOTHER OF TWO, AGES 8 AND 5.

# How Pricing Affects Moms' Purchases

OUR SURVEY RESULTS illustrate that pricing plays a role in marketing to mothers. In advertising it is an important contributing factor to the effectiveness of the ad. Forty-nine percent of mothers said that price-focused ads are very effective and another forty percent said they are somewhat effective. We asked mothers, "When making buying decisions, how much influence do coupons, advertised specials, loyalty programs, special members, special events, or information found in doctors' offices play in your decision of where to shop?" Over 50 percent said that advertised specials very much influence them, while another 45 percent said discount coupons produce the same buying behavior.

Q. *What part does pricing play in where you shop and what you purchase?*

A. "Pricing plays an important part of my purchases in every area but one. Although I know I could save money by clipping coupons or shopping more wisely, I tend not to place an importance on price when it comes to food. I am very price sensitive with children's stuff because I know they will either grow out of it or it will be destroyed before too long. The life of the product is short whether I buy for quality or value. I think Target has found a way for moms to have style and economy. I buy something for the kids there knowing it might not last forever but it will be stylish and cute for the time they wear it."

MEG, MOTHER OF TWO, AGES 8 AND 6.

A. "Vary rarely am I persuaded to try a new product unless there is a price incentive or a friend recommends a product that she has tried."

BECKY, MOTHER OF TWO, AGES 8 AND 5.

A. "If I find a product I like for my family, I stick with it, but if I find it on sale, I will stock up on it. If a newspaper ad intrigues me with a specially priced item, I will try the item if it's being sold at a store I tend to frequent. I cut coupons, but don't tend to use them often."

CATHY, MOTHER OF THREE, AGES 10, 8, AND 5.

# Trusting the Doctor

AN INTERESTING RESULT emerged about the influence of materials in a doctor's office. Over fifty-five percent of mothers said they are somewhat influenced by information they find in their doctor's office.

$Q.$ *How likely are you to be influenced by materials found in your doctor's office?*

$A.$ "Occasionally I pick up product information at the doctor's office. I believe there are a number of factors at work here. The first is that we all have to wait so much in the doctor's office! I also believe that, for the most part, if women find information in their doctor's offices, they have a tendency to trust that information and the company providing it more—especially if they trust their doctor."

TAMMY, MOTHER OF FOUR, AGES 6, 4, 2, AND 1.

$A.$ "During a recent wellness check for one of my daughters, I asked my pediatrician about a new ADHD product, Metadate CD. We discussed the pros and cons, and his recommendation to try it. Any hesitation I might have had disappeared when he told me he'd give me a coupon good for a free thirty-day product sample. We agreed to talk after three weeks to see how my daughter adjusted to it. It worked for me—I trusted his recommendation and appreciated trying it for free. And, best of all, it worked for my daughter."

DOROTHY, MOTHER OF TWO, AGE 9 (TWINS).

$A.$ "When I am waiting in the reception room, I do check out the materials about products in the waiting room and might ask the doctor about a certain product that appeals to me. I think a doctor's office is a good place to get to moms because mostly it's 'mom' who takes the child to the doctor when necessary. Advertisers have a captive audience when moms are waiting in the waiting room."

NANCY, MOTHER OF TWO, AGES 17 AND 10.

## Sample Items and Demonstrations

MOTHERS LIKE TO touch and feel product and having the opportunity to do so influences their buying decisions. Samples are reaching mothers not only through mail campaigns but also at special events and in-store demonstrations. Each is equally appealing and effective in driving a mother's buying behavior.

**Q.** *Are you more likely to purchase a product you see demonstrated or sampled?*

**A.** "I am more likely to purchase new things for my home if I have had an opportunity to see it operate or had a chance to taste it. I think of Costco samples. As a working mom, I have developed an appreciation for simplicity . . . things that are easy to operate, have few pieces to assemble, or food that is nutritious and easily prepared. If a vendor is able to demonstrate that they meet any of these needs, I am likely to give their product a try."

SHARON, MOTHER OF THREE, AGES 10, 9, AND 7.

**A.** "I am likely to buy a product that I see demonstrated or sampled if it is already on my shopping list. I think being able to touch and taste a product before buying it allows mothers to make a better decision on a purchase so that the toy or food item will not be wasted when they take it home to their kids. Also, when a company gives samples, it seems they have confidence in their product."

CHRIS, MOTHER OF TWO, AGES 3 YEARS AND 9 MONTHS.

**A.** "I am more apt to buy something I see demonstrated or displayed when it comes to fashion. I am very visual and hands-on, so taste, texture, and seeing something in motion really works for me. It reduces any skepticism I might have in the product."

ANNE, MOTHER OF TWO, AGES 2 YEARS AND 2 MONTHS.

**A.** "The Sunday newspaper this past week included a new nutritional health bar specifically made for women. The package stated that it was loaded with soy protein, beta-carotene, vitamins, etc. I tasted it and really enjoyed it. I plan to purchase them this week when I go to the grocery store. I think that offering a free sample of a product or service is so important in marketing especially if you are offering something new. I would never think to buy the nutritional bar if I just saw the box in the grocery aisle."

JULIE, MOTHER OF FOUR, AGES 6, 5, AND 3 (TWINS).

## What Working Mothers Want

WE ASKED THOSE mothers who were employed about their role and attitudes as a working mom. In order to set the stage for their responses about work and family benefits, it is important to recognize that almost 50 percent of them have full-time childcare outside of the home. The others responded that they have some variation of in-home care or a part-time provider to aid in their childcare solutions.

We asked our working mothers to reflect on their attitudes toward working-mother benefits being offered by employers in general. Their answers did not have to be associated with benefits that they receive from their employer, but rather how important they think certain benefits are to all working mothers. Over 95 percent said that flextime was extremely or very important as a benefit for working moms. Paid and partially paid health insurance ranked second and third on the list, earning over 80 percent of the vote. Flexible schedules and health insurance outranked childcare assistance and compensation by over 20 percentage points.

**Q.** *What work/life benefits are most important to you as a working mother?*

**A.** "Flexibility is the best benefit an employer can offer me because my husband's company provides us health insurance. . . . Flex time would allow me to go on a class field trip or be home with my child if he is sick without having to worry that my employer is upset. While my child is young, I would value a flexible schedule over an increase in pay or a promotion."

CHRIS, MOTHER OF ONE, AGE 8.

**A.** "The flexibility to allow me to positively interact with all my children's activities. My children are only young once so I want to be able to have the flexibility to experience with them all the things that are molding them in the adults they will grow up to be. I would put flexibility above pay at this stage of my parenthood."

ROBIN, MOTHER OF THREE, AGES 8 YEARS,
4 YEARS, AND 10 MONTHS.

# What Working Mothers Get

WHEN WE ASKED working mothers which benefits were offered within their own company, over 60 percent said they are given the opportunity for a flexible schedule and just over half received some type of health insurance payment. Our working mothers are split as to the goals of their companies in marketing themselves to mothers as employees. Just over one-third responded that their employer consistently works toward making policy changes to assist working mothers. Another third said that their employer has very little concern for the problems of working mothers, and just under a third said that their employer considers changes that will assist working mothers but rarely implements them. Mothers agree that companies are not doing enough to talk about what they are doing for working mothers. When asked if their employer promotes itself in the community as being a working-mother friendly company, over 70 percent said no.

**Q.** *Do you think employers are doing enough to make changes for working mothers?*

**A.** "No, employers need to be more open to flex time and telecommuting. Sometimes the demands of the traditional nine-to-five structure can be restricting to a mother. It doesn't mean that they can't be a productive employee if their work hours are something different. . . . A valuable employee is valuable at any time."

MARTI, MOTHER OF ONE, AGE 2.

**A.** "I think companies have come further in trying to help working mothers. I personally think that it is more than a working-mother issue; companies have to recognize working parents. Flexibility is very important and companies need to be more creative in coming up with ways to allow parents to participate in their children's activities. It's not only good for the parents but for society as a whole. I think on-site day cares are a wonderful benefit and one that should be applauded."

BRENDA, MOTHER OF THREE, AGES
8 YEARS, 5 YEARS, AND NEWBORN.

■   ■   ■

The results of our research clearly show that many opportunities exist for marketers to capture a greater share of the spending power of mothers. From what you have read in this chapter, you should be able to fully appreciate the marketing potential that mothers represent. Mothers are online, reading magazines, sending e-mails, and talking to each other a lot. What they aren't doing is connecting with advertising. Moms have told us that there is an enormous opportunity to speak to them in a meaningful manner. They have also told us that when we do earn their business they will stay with us in order to save time.

## CHAPTER THIRTEEN

# Pushing the Stroller to Opportunity

WHEN A NEW mother receives her baby in her arms for the first time, she wonders if she will know how to care for the precious bundle she has been given. Every mother silently questions her ability to figure out the needs of her baby. This universal feeling of doubt is a popular subject on evening sitcoms. The scene is usually a mother and father trying to figure out what a baby wants while the baby continues to cry regardless of the actions of the parents.

As a marketer or advertiser, you share more with the mom market than you realize. View your role as that of a mother. Your child is the mom market, a bundle of opportunities waiting for you to take it to its full potential. Each time you launch a marketing campaign that generates incremental sales or strengthens your brand, you are taking your market to a new level. Just as a mother may have to use different styles of parenting for each of her children, you must determine the best approach to connect with your segment of the mom market.

We talked about the importance of walking in the shoes of your market. A mother knows that if you truly listen to a child, he will tell you what he needs. It's time for you to listen to your child—the mom market. In chapter 12 we heard from our bundle of opportunity. Moms told us what they liked about advertising and where opportunities for change exist. Now let's use all we know and apply it to meeting the needs of our child. Let's push the stroller toward opportunity.

# Tapping into the Mom Market: Examining Four Key Results

A GOOD PLACE to start tapping into the mom market is to examine the four key results from our conversation with mothers. First is the fact that 80 percent of the mom market thinks print advertising is only doing an okay to not-okay-at-all job in speaking to moms. Second, only 25 percent of mothers think television advertising is doing a good job connecting with the mom market. Third, only 38 percent of mothers feel that companies recognize and acknowledge the needs of mothers in their advertising campaigns. Finally, over 50 percent of moms said that they see ads often or very often that send the wrong message to moms.

This is obviously a chance to differentiate your brand. There is an enormous opportunity to rise above all the marketing clutter that is missing the target. You can do this by applying the lessons learned in this book. Clearly define the segment of the mom market you intend to target with your marketing plan. Use the right forms of communication to reach that market, and deliver a message that is relevant and valued by the moms who see it. Take the time to look at the colored mosaics that make up your target market (as was suggested by Bonnie Ulman of The Haystack Group) and determine her life stage and parenting style. This will determine the language you are going to speak to her. We saw in our research that mothers want you to communicate with benefits and solutions and with graphics that mimic their lives.

As was pointed out by Denise Fedewa of LeoBurnett, we need to remember that mothers have a sense of humor and don't aspire to be a mother of the 1950s. Leave the June Cleaver images in the closet where they belong. Moms are smart, savvy, and emotional beings that care about the safety and well-being of their families. As Dr. Gail Gross said earlier, "You can't cut a mother off at the neck." And, as we learned in our research, you can't cut out their wallets either. Mothers apply pricing and value to obtaining happiness in products and services for their families.

# Getting on the Same Playing Field

THE NEXT OPPORTUNITY that is present in the mom market is location. To get our newly revised message to mothers, we have to be on their playing field.

## THE IMPORTANCE OF MAGAZINES

Although moms split their media time between television, radio, and newspapers, they find more time to read magazines. In fact, they find the time to read or flip through the pages of numerous titles during the month. You have the opportunity to relay your marketing message as a mother spends time with a magazine. Magazines are a place that she turns to find solutions for everyday challenges. She is also more likely to buy a product if it appears in an article than if she sees it in an advertisement.

Take this opportunity to reevaluate media placements. Although national magazine advertising is expensive and is known to work only with frequency, the results may warrant reallocating funds to reach your market of mothers. Don't discount the availability of zone rates or remnant pricing, which can allow modest budgets to advertise in national titles. Inquire about the household makeup of the publication's circulation prior to placing ads. We know that mothers take the time to read magazines, but make sure you are advertising in the magazines your mom market is reading. Also take into consideration the extended shelf life of the publication and design your ad according to the lessons and language we have discussed already. Design your ads to be clean, clear, and quick.

## THE DOCTOR'S OFFICE

Let's revisit the doctor's office for a minute. It's not only patients waiting at the pediatrician's office, opportunity is sitting there, too. Moms told us that they are more likely to buy a product if they see information about it in their physician's office or he or she recommends it. Here you have a chance to speak to a captive mother with creatively integrated messaging while she cares for the health of her child. Your strategy could be to provide stickers or colorful pencils with your company's name on them for the nurse to give to children. Or have available company-sponsored items such as growth charts or attractive, solution-oriented brochures sitting on the tables in the waiting room. Moms told us that sampling is an effective way to win their attention, and this is the perfect place to initiate such a marketing campaign. What could be more compelling than a doctor handing your product to a prospective customer?

## Online

Moms told us that they are spending time online. When we combine this with their desire to find answers, save time, and converse with other moms, the Internet presents many avenues to connect with the mom market. Our moms' responses validate that companies such as Nestle's VeryBestMeals.com, VeryBestBaby.com, and BabyUniverse.com are right in executing an Internet strategy that saves a mother time and offers her valuable information. Moms also told us that Stork Avenue.com and eBubbles.com are doing the right thing in maximizing their exposure on search engines because that's how half of moms find sites. The other half agreed that firms like BlueSuitMom.com, who are including their URL in all printed ads, are reaching their market. Finally, almost a third of moms said e-mail was a good way to reach them with your advertising message.

Companies can maximize online potential by using electronic e-mails that present helpful information, top-ten lists that reduce the amount of time it takes to research a topic, and interactive tools that help mothers simplify their daily life. Forty-two percent of mothers said they talked to other moms about products and services via e-mail. By including marketing initiatives that reward and encourage moms to share your information online with others, you can be a part of these valuable conversations, too.

## RADIO

Radio offers another opportunity to talk to mothers. The car is a second home to many as they shuttle children from school to activities. Whether it is through exclusively designed programming or on-air advertising, radio provides access to a captive audience. It is an underutilized medium that provides a cost-effective way to speak to moms.

## AT WORK

We learned that the potential of the mom market is carried in a briefcase as well as a diaper bag. Moms play an important role in controlling the overall spending in offices as well as households. Companies who recognize the significance of mothers as business owners and purchasing agents will reap the benefits of mothers as consumers.

# Becoming Mom-Friendly from Top to Bottom

IF THE MOTHERS who are closest to you, your employees, do not see you as mom-friendly, your customers outside the company certainly won't view you as such either. The message must start from within.

Mothers told us that companies like Liz Claiborne and Avon are doing the right thing by offering flexible schedules, day-care solutions, and career opportunities to women. Employers who offer these benefits profit as well, with increased productivity, positive morale, and employee retention. Flexible schedules rank high in the minds of mothers, which means that companies who take the time to set new policies have the opportunity to realize new levels of employment loyalty. Flextime is an inexpensive solution to the expensive problem of employee turnover.

If you feel like you are offering desirable work/family benefits, check with your employees to make sure you are successfully communicating your commitment. Remember, 70 percent of working mothers said companies did not do a good job promoting themselves as a family-friendly company. It's just as important to *communicate* the message of having the benefits as it is to deliver them. Don't miss out on the opportunity to attract valuable talent by keeping your work/family benefits a secret. Would you leave a product's benefit out of a print ad? Don't leave it out of your employment ads either.

## Cultivating Loyalty

THE QUEST FOR a mom's buying decision will pay off. Moms told us that they are loyal to the products that serve them well. To tap into the potential moms represent, companies should have specific quality controls and customer retention elements within their marketing plans. Mothers will stay loyal to companies who provide good customer service, which includes fulfilling product promises, on-time delivery, and clear return policies. Good customer service translates to saving time and creating convenience for mothers, very valuable commodities.

Mothers also like to be appreciated; rewarding their loyalty intensifies it. Rewards can be as simple as special savings, communications, services, or shopping hours. In the eyes of a mother, the gesture is worth even more than the action.

# The Ideal Marketing Plan?

WE'D ALL LOVE to find that magic marketing plan that will allow us to capture the trillions being spent by mothers. No such plan exists, but if someone had an unlimited budget to apply to the insights we have gained in this book, their plan might read like this:

- Initiate a strong publicity campaign to get articles written about my product in magazines.
- Provide product samples to doctors and pediatricians.
- Create ads that highlight product benefits.
- Position my product as a solution to a problem.
- Design a Web site that provides timesaving interactive tools.
- Send valuable e-mail messages.
- Find or create a place on the radio dial with solution-oriented programming.
- Launch an employee program with flextime for my employees.
- Incorporate women business owners into my vendor lists.
- Create television ads that are relevant to all mothers.
- Host special events that provide information and demonstrate products.
- Distribute premiums with long shelf life to children.
- Reward the loyalty of my customers.
- Train my employees to support marketing and deliver superb customer service.

It looks like a good plan at first glance. The problem with this marketing strategy, however, is that it doesn't take into consideration the individual qualities of mothers, the application of the product to their lives, and the many other mosaics that create the niches of the mom market. The solution to tapping into the buying power of moms just can't be found in a one-size-fits-all marketing plan. Moms are just as unique as the marketing plan you need to reach your market.

In order to capture your piece of the trillion-dollar mom market, you must take what you've learned here and create the plan that is right for you and your target market. You hold the baby, you have the tools, and now it's up to you to take your market from infancy to maturity. A trillion dollars of spending is waiting out there for you.

# Notes

## Introduction

1. Harris Interactive, *The Online Woman: How to Tap into Her Buying Power* (1999), www.harrisinteractive.com.
2. Amey Stone, "Not Much to Nurture Moms on the Net," *Business Week* (Sept. 15, 2000).
3. Young & Rubicam, "The Intelligence Factory," *The Single Female Consumer* (Young & Rubicam, July 2000), www.yr.com.
4. Center for Women's Business Research, *Women-Owned Business in the United States, 2002: A Fact Sheet* (Washington, D.C.: Center for Women's Business Research, 2002), www.nfwbo.org.
5. Ibid.
6. Connie Glaser, "The Women's Market Rules," *Competitive Edge* (May/June 2001).
7. U.S. Bureau of Labor Statistics, *Working in the Twenty-first Century* (Washington, D.C., 2000).
8. Ibid.
9. James Bennet, "Soccer Mom 2000," *New York Times* (April 9, 2002).
10. U.S. Department of Agriculture, *Expenditures on Children by Families* (Washington, D.C.: GPO, June 2001).
11. Ibid.

12. Census Bureau, *Population Projections of the Untied States by Age, Sex, and Race: 1995 to 2050* (Washington, D.C.: GPO, 2000), www.census.gov.

13. Center for Women's Business Research.

14. Ibid.

15. Ibid.

16. Connie Glaser.

17. Faith Popcorn, *EVEolution: Understand Women: Eight Essential Truths That Work in Your Business and Life* (New York: Hyperion, 2001).

## Chapter 1

1. Mark Lino, "Expenditures on Children by Families," U.S. Department of Agriculture, Center for Nutrition Policy and Promotion, 2001 annual report. Miscellaneous Publication No. 1528-2001.

2. Center for Women's Business Research, *Women-Owned Business in the United States, 2002: A Fact* Sheet (Washington, D.C.: Center for Women's Business Research, 2002), www.nfwbo.org.

3. Census Bureau, *Characteristics of Unmarried Partners and Married Spouses by Sex* (Washington, D.C.: GPO, March 2000), www.census.gov.

4. Ibid.

5. Ibid.

6. S. J. Ventura and C. A. Bachrach, "Nonmarital Childbearing in the United States, 1940–1999," *National Vital Statistics Reports* 48, no. 16 (Hyattsville, MD: National Center for Health Statistics, 2000).

7. Center for Women's Business Research.

8. Rebecca Gardyn, "The Home Front," *American Demographics* 23, no. 12 (December 2001): 34.

## Chapter 2

1. Robert Lavidge and Gary Stiener, "A Model for the Predictive Measurement of Advertising Effectiveness," *Journal of Marketing* (October 1961).

2. Radcliffe Public Policy Center, *Life's Work: Generational Attitudes Toward Work and Life Integration* (Cambridge, MA: Radcliffe Public Policy Center, May 3, 2000).

## Chapter 3

1. Census Bureau, *Characteristics of Unmarried Partners and Married Spouses by Sex* (Washington, D.C.: GPO, March 2000).

2. U.S. Bureau of Labor Statistics, *2001 Statistical Abstract of the United States* (Washington, D.C.: GPO, January 2002).

3. Center for Women's Business Research, *Women-Owned Businesses in the United States, 2002: A Fact Sheet* (Washington, D.C.: Center for Women's Business Research, 2002), www.nfwbo.org.

4. Ibid.

5. Center for Women's Business Research, *The Characteristics and Contributions of Home-Based Women-Owned Businesses in the United States* (Washington, D.C.: Center for Women's Business Research, November 16, 1995), www.nfwbo.org.

6. Catalyst, "The Next Generation: Today's Professionals, Tomorrow's Leaders," (December 11, 2001), www.catalyst women.org.

7. 9to5 National Association of Working Women, *Women in the Workforce: Highlights of the 9to5 Profile of Working Women 2000* (Washington, D.C.: 9to5 National Association of Working Women, 2000), www.9to5.org/profile.html.

8. Ibid.

9. Whirlpool Foundation Study, *Women: The New Providers* (Benton Harbor, MI: Whirlpool Foundation, 1995).

10. Ibid.

11. Ibid.

12. National Center for Education Statistics, *Parent Survey of the National Household Education Surveys Program, Table 1* (Washington, D.C.: National Center for Education Statistics, 1999).

13. Census Bureau.

## Chapter 4

1. Surface Transportation Policy Project, *High Mileage Moms* (Washington, D.C.: Surface Transportation Policy Project, May 6, 1999).

2. Ibid.

## Chapter 5

1. Pew Internet and American Life Project, "Women Surpass Men As E-Shoppers During the Holidays" (January 1, 2001), www.pewinternet.org.

2. Nielsen Media Research, "TV Viewing in Internet Households" (May 1999), www.nielsenmedia.com.

3. Cyber Dialogue, "Cyber Dialogue finds women reluctant to shop online due to security issues" (Press release published on www.cyberdialogue.com, January 2001).

4. Ibid.

5. Michael Pastore, "Security Keeps Women from Shopping Online" (Cyberatlas.com, January 10, 2000).

## Chapter 6

1. Michael K. Bergman, *The Deep Web: Surfacing Hidden Value* (http://brightplanet.com, July 26, 2000).

## Chapter 7

1. Data provided to author by the National Mail Order Association.

## Chapter 9

1. Census Bureau 2000, Summary File 1, Matrices P13 and PCT 12, www.factfinder.census.gov.

2. James McNeal, *The Kids' Market: Myths and Realities* (Promotional Resource Group, June 1999), www.kidstuff.com.

3. Susan Linn, "Electronic Marketing: 'Here, Kiddie, Kiddie!' The Hours That Children Devote to TV," *Boston Globe* (January 16, 2000).

4. Ibid.

5. Eli Lambert, Leah Plunkett, and Trish Wotowiec, *Just the Facts about Advertising and Marketing to Children* (Takoma Park, MD: The Center for a New American Dream, 2002).

6. Laurie Klein, "More Than Play Dough," *Brandweek* 38, (November 24, 1997).

7. Lambert, Plunkett, Wotowiec.

8. Ibid.

## Chapter 10

1. Susan Harrow, "How to Get on Oprah," www.prsecretstore .com/ultimateguide.html.

## Chapter 11

1. U.S. Bureau of Labor Statistics, *2001 Statistical Abstract of the United States* (Washington, D.C.: GPO, January 2002).

2. National Association of Female Executives, *Top Twenty-Five Companies for Female Executives* (New York: National Association of Female Executives, 2001).

3. Report published online at www.nfwbo.org.

4. "Replacement Therapy," *Executive Female* (February/March 2002): 26.

5. Work and Family Connection, *Work and Family Trend Report: Some of the Decade's Most Important Studies* (Minnetonka, MN: Work and Family Connection, 1999).

6. U.S. Bureau of Labor Statistics, *Occupational Quarterly Outlook* (Washington, D.C.: GPO, June 2000).

7. U.S. Bureau of Labor Statistics, *Monthly Labor Review* (Washington, D.C.: GPO, June 2000).

8. Radcliffe Public Policy Center, *Life's Work: Generational Attitudes Toward Work and Life Integration* (Cambridge, MA: Radcliffe Public Policy Center, May 3, 2000).

9. *Working Mother* media kit, November 1999.

10. Catalyst, *2000 Catalyst Census of Women Corporate Officers and Top Earners of the Fortune 500* (Catalyst, 2000), www.catalyst women.org.

11. Center for Women's Business Research, *Key Facts* (Washington, D.C.: Center for Women's Business Research, 2001).

# Index _____